# PRAISE FOR THE PLAYS OF HALLEY FEIFFER

## HOW TO MAKE FRIENDS AND THEN KILL THEM

"Ms. Feiffer . . . is building a reputation for fearlessness."

—Neil Genzlinger, *The New York Times*

"Thank God . . . for the warped creative mind of playwright/actress Halley Feiffer, who harnesses the weird to full, gory effect in *How to Make Friends and Then Kill Them,* an uproarious and deeply unsettling new dark comedy . . . Equally laugh-out-loud funny, jaw-droppingly gross, and thoroughly sad . . . Feiffer's unique, refreshing voice is one to which attention should be paid."

—David Gordon, *Theatermania*

"Disturbingly funny."

—Joe Dziemianowicz, *New York Daily News*

"A wicked comedy . . . Feiffer . . . is an expert comic actor with an appealingly skewed sensibility."

—Elisabeth Vincentelli, *New York Post*

"Feiffer . . . has a commendable eye for the absurd."

—*The New Yorker*

"There's great stuff here . . . dark and weird."

—*Time Out New York*

## I'M GONNA PRAY FOR YOU SO HARD

"Viciously funny . . . brutally effective. Feiffer takes a tough look at the forces that can bring us to our knees."

—Adam Feldman, *Time Out New York*

"A bone-chilling . . . punishing drama."

—Charles Isherwood, *The New York Times*

**HALLEY FEIFFER** is a New York-based writer and actress. Her full-length plays include *I'm Gonna Pray For You So Hard* (World Premiere Atlantic Theater Company, 2015), *How To Make Friends And Then Kill Them* (World Premiere Rattlestick Playwrights Theater, 2014), and *A Funny Thing Happened On The Way To The Gynecologic Oncology Unit At Memorial Sloan-Kettering Cancer Center of New York City* (World Premiere MCC Theater, 2016). Her plays have been developed by Manhattan Theatre Club, Second Stage, New York Theater Workshop, LAByrinth Theater Company, The O'Neill, and elsewhere. She holds commissions from Manhattan Theatre Club, The Alfred P. Sloan Foundation, Williamstown Theater Festival, Jen Hoguet Productions, and Playwrights Horizons. She co-wrote and starred in the 2013 film *He's Way More Famous Than You* and co-created and stars in the web series *What's Your Emergency*. She is a writer on the Starz series *The One Percent*.

# I'M GONNA PRAY FOR YOU SO HARD

A PLAY BY

## HALLEY FEIFFER

OVERLOOK DUCKWORTH
New York • London

This edition first published in the United States and the United Kingdom in 2015 by Overlook Duckworth, Peter Mayer Publishers, Inc.

NEW YORK
141 Wooster Street
New York, NY 10012
www.overlookpress.com
For bulk and special sales, please contact sales@overlookny.com,
or write us at above address.

LONDON
30 Calvin Street
London E1 6NW
info@duckworth-publishers.co.uk
www.ducknet.co.uk
For bulk and special sales, please contact sales@duckworth-publishers.co.uk,
or write us at the above address.

Cataloging-in-Publication Data is available from the Library of Congress
A catalogue record for this book is available from the British Library

*Book design and type formatting by Bernard Schleifer*
Manufactured in the United States of America
ISBN 978-1-4683-1108-2 (US)
ISBN 978-0-7156-5018-9 (UK)
3 5 7 9 10 8 6 4 2

# I'M GONNA PRAY
# FOR YOU SO HARD

# PREFACE

A young actress, Ella, has just opened in a production of *The Seagull*, and some hours later, in the wee hours of the night, is in her playwright father's kitchen on the Upper West Side of Manhattan (ahh the Upper West Side, home to world-weary artists of a certain generation, to refugees from the old world, exiles and psychiatrists, Jewish intellectuals, and so on, all virtually extinct), all of whose children have fled now for Brooklyn, the coast, or at least somewhere below Houston Street.

Because children flee their parents, as they must, as they should, in order to become whatever they must be.

Not, however, Ella, the actress in question.

In her mid 20s at least, she is still a captive to her father's opinions and decrees, which tonight spew forth from his mouth in an endless fountain not of youth but of vitriol, spleen, and rage. (Along the lines of "You're too good for the role of Masha / you shoulda been Nina / but the production was terrible anyway, the director is a hack, AND he was too busy to direct my last play.") And THIS father knows from the theatre; what with his aging Pulitzer on the shelf, endless anecdotes about how he came up, and a paucity of new ideas, grace, or generosity, he is THE authority, the final word, the bottom line—when it comes to passing judgment on his daughter and her nascent life in the now dead and useless American theatre, which he feels has spit him out like a husk. And thus begins Halley Feiffer's brilliant and harrowing play about art and life in the theatre, fathers and daughters, and the making of clever little monsters.

*I'm Gonna Pray For You So Hard* dives long and deep into a spectacularly dangerous and ill-lit pool—a final night, as it were, of the soul for a young artist who can barely keep up with her father's coke, screeds, and weed use but tries gamely, while in the other room, the young actress's mother, a silent party, a totem and victim, has retired for the night but can still hear the laughter and venom wafting into the bedroom from the kitchen where the action all goes down. And then in Act 2, the play changes course to explore the dire, inevitable consequences of that night and so many nights like it, from a distance of some years on. Ella has by then become a hardened thing of New York—well armored, brittle, and fueled by the same mind-altering substances, replaying the old deadly songs she sang with her dad, but in a far lower key.

Joan Didion famously observed, "Writers are always selling somebody out." I don't know if that's true—if for instance, the "always" *always* applies—but I accept the premise that a writer has to have some delicately honed listening devices always in use, always recording, like some omnipresent, undetectable NSA system floating in deep space. Writers need memories as long as they are flawed, and they need to accept those flaws because it is only in the flaws that we find the components to make art. A play like Halley's is born in the liminal spaces between narrative and memory, where fog and haze distort our vision. It is only in sifting through our worst nights and the lies we are complicit in during them that the betrayal Ms. Didion speaks of becomes more valuable than a petty act of literary revenge.

Halley Feiffer may be the daughter of a famous playwright, but what she has done with that small statement of *fact* is to turn it inside out, doing what all writers, what all artists must do; using the repository of memory to cannibalize mood, lifting out bits of film from the old cans, clips from the weird home movies we carry inside, playing them over and over, peering at the stills, the scents and textures we call "recollection," to make something whole and complete and her own.

What so compelled me toward her play was that I recognized that, like me, she is trying to sift through the particles and debris from prior crash sites in her own life. Trying to become somewhat better: a better thinker, a better writer, a more whole being; someone capable of conjuring up a recognizable and yet original world. I also think plays can be warnings to their authors, canaries in the coal mine in some inchoate prescriptive sense. (An example—in my play, *The Film Society*, a very early play, I see the outline of a terrible future in an awful past, one in which my weakness becomes so deadly that it costs people around me everything. I have, over the years, tried to

avoid becoming the central character in that play, which I only identi-
fied in the first place by writing the thing.)

Watching *I'm Gonna Pray For You So Hard*, I ruminated that, in
the theatre, writers are so much like actors—we use memory as a
fire accelerant to create a long enough incantation, a sustained deep-
enough spell, and one that can stay alive for long enough so that we
can at the very least just name it, and by so doing have some power
over it. The spell must have a name. In this case it is called *I'm
Gonna Pray For You So Hard*.

I think I loved this spell so much because it would not let me go,
and because it was ruthless and hard and punishing and, in fact,
because it was so hard and punishing, the play broke through a bar-
rier before evaporating, and what was left after the smoke had
cleared in my brain was the outline of a very bright future for its self-
flagellating creator.

Jon Robin Baitz
April 2015

# ACKNOWLEDGMENTS

This play would not exist if it were not for my fearless collaborator and friend Trip Cullman, who championed it from the very beginning and who has been vital in shaping it into what it is today. My reverence for his mind is boundless.

Enormous gratitude to our World Premiere cast, the peerless Reed Birney and Betty Gilpin, who have taught and inspired me more than I can say, and whose contribution to this play has been invaluable.

Massive thanks to Neil Pepe, who produced the World Premiere of this play at the Atlantic Theater Company, overseeing its development with unparalleled compassion and support. And to Annie MacRae, who was one of this play's first champions, and without whose enthusiasm and keen eye this play would be merely a shadow of its current self.

I am so grateful for my agent Di Glazer—the hardest working woman in show business, and a perfect partner in crime.

Thank you to everyone who has so generously contributed to the development of this play since its infancy: John Guare, Michael Padden, Austin Pendleton, Kate Dalton, Louis Cancelmi, The Rattlestick Playwrights Theater, David Van Asselt, Brian Roff, Lyle Kessler, Rosal Colon, Katherine Waterston, Stephen Adly Guirgis, LAByrinth Theater Company, Kenneth Lonergan, Chris Burney, Michael Esper, Second Stage Theater, Peter Friedman, Manhattan Theater Club, Mandy Greenfield, The Eugene O'Neill Theater Center, The NTI Theatermakers (Summer '14), Wendy Goldberg, Preston Whiteway, Thomas Kail, Jessica Amato, The Atlantic Theater Company, Jaime Castañeda, Christian Parker, Abigail Katz, Jeffory Lawson, Teresa Gozzo, Jenna Ready, Douglas Healy, Amy Crossman, Daniel Kluger, Jessica Pabst, Ben Stanton, Mark Wendland, Rebecca Azenberg, Caroline Schreiber, Colleen Heaney, Lori Ann Zepp, Jon Robin Baitz, Di Glazer, Jenny Allen and Jules Feiffer.

# PRODUCTION CREDITS

The World Premiere of *I'm Gonna Pray For You So Hard* was presented by Atlantic Theater Company, New York City, 2015. Directed by Trip Cullman.

**ELLA**         Betty Gilpin

**DAVID**       Reed Birney


*I'm Gonna Pray For You So Hard* was developed during a residency at the Eugene O'Neill Theater Center's National Playwrights Conference in 2014.

Preston Whiteway                    Wendy C. Goldberg
Executive Director                    Artistic Director

# THE CHARACTERS

**ELLA**: Twenties. An up-and-coming actress.

**DAVID**: Seventies. A famous playwright. Ella's father.

# SETTING

ACT I: An Upper West Side Manhattan apartment. Present day.

ACT II: A downtown New York City black box theater. Five years later.

# SCENE I

*An enormous eat-in kitchen in a large but gone-to-seed prewar apartment on the Upper West Side. Late at night.*

*The room is a mess—papers and books clutter the table; half empty wine bottles dot every surface; overflowing ashtrays and old plates of crusty leftovers are scattered about.*

ELLA *and* DAVID *sit at the table.*

ELLA *wears no makeup. She wears loose-fitting shorts and a flannel shirt. Her hair is pulled back into a ponytail.*

DAVID *has scraggly gray hair and gray stubble. He wears outdated coke-bottle glasses, rumpled khaki pants with ink stains on the pockets, and a wrinkled button-down shirt with the top few buttons unbuttoned, revealing white chest hair.*

*They both drink white wine with ice. The recently-opened magnum bottle is on the table. They both smoke cigarettes. They are in the middle of a heated conversation.*

DAVID

See that's what I'm talking about—they're all fucking idiots—

ELLA

I know, I know—

DAVID

No you *don't* know, Ella! Let me finish—

ELLA

Sorry—

DAVID

They are a sick cadre of pathetic, sniveling, *tiny* men with *micropenises* and *no* imaginations who write out of their asses and who *love* to tear you down because in truth they know that you are doing *exactly* what they could never do—that you are doing the only thing they have ever *wanted* to do—and they are fucking *jealous*. You know that, don't you? How jealous they are? They're *boiling* with envy. They want a *piece* of you. They want in. They wanna get *inside* you! They wanna *climb right in!*

ELLA

(*Laughing.*)

Whoa!

DAVID

I'm *serious*. They wanna *fuck* you. They wanna fuck you so hard, they're *blind* with fuck-rage.

ELLA

(*Mesmerized.*)

Wow!

DAVID

*Yes.* "Wow" is right! And even though they're almost exclusively queers—you think that matters? It doesn't matter! Because the kind of fucking they wanna do to you is gender-blind, soul-blind—they're blind to it themselves!

ELLA

Right!

DAVID

I mean it's like a fucking snot-nosed kid dipping your braid in his *inkwell!* They get a kind of pleasure out of being *perverse*.

ELLA

HAH!

DAVID

I'm not kidding. Why are you laughing?

ELLA

I'm not—

DAVID

It's like a pedophile and his *prey!* Humbert Humbert and Lolita! She obsesses him and this disgusts him so he abuses her and then he *fucks* her, and then abuses her and then *fucks* her again!

ELLA

Yes—*yes!*

DAVID

I mean haven't you realized it's always the *brilliant* performances that are the ones that go unnoticed—or even worse!—the ones that get the kind of condescending, bullshit mentions like: "The *serviceable* Ella Berryman."

ELLA

Oh god.

DAVID

"The capable . . ."

ELLA

"The reliable . . ."

DAVID

"The sturdy . . .!" As if you're a fucking *stool* they enjoyed *sitting* on for the evening!

ELLA

I know—I *know!*

DAVID

Or even worse: just the name, in *parentheses*—"When Medvedenko professes his love to Masha"—and then in parentheses: "(Ella Berryman),"—

ELLA

Oh god! The *worst!*

DAVID

Oh god, and *then!* What's even *worse!* Just to rub some salt in the wound—just really *grind* it in—after giving you the requisite, dismissive nod—"Ella Berryman", (close paren)—*then*, a paragraph later they'll say: "Well, the *real* pleasure of the evening is the *exquisite* performance of—"

ELLA

*(Loving this.)*
Oh god—just *stop!* Just stop right there!

DAVID

And then they pick the *one person* in the cast who's a fucking *hack!*

ELLA

(Giggling.)
Of course—of *course!*

DAVID

The one actor who's chewing the scenery as if he just got fucking *dentures* and he's getting executed next *Tuesday!*

ELLA

(Laughing.)
I know—I *know!*

DAVID

Or the "*ingenue*"—the girl who's sexy, or (maybe more accurately), what a gay man thinks he's *supposed* to think is sexy—

ELLA

Ugh, like *Clementine.*

DAVID

Exactly! Like that fucking *Clementine* in your play! (*Ironically.*) Your perfect little "Nina" . . . .

ELLA

Oh gross. *Gross!*

DAVID

But that's exactly what they *want!* A wide-eyed, little brain-dead . . . *trout*-mouth who clearly only a man *terrified* of his own mor*tality* would want to fuck!

ELLA

(Suddenly very sad.)
But *everyone* wants to fuck her. . . .

DAVID

Well everyone fucking *hates* themselves!

ELLA

(Giggling.)
That's true—that's *true!*

DAVID

That's why Bertrand cast her, didn't he? We know that, don't we? I mean, it's certainly not because she's a good fucking *actress!*

ELLA

*(Laughing.)*

No!

DAVID

It's not because of her emotional *depth!*

ELLA

Right!

DAVID

Her *subtlety!*

ELLA

Hah!

DAVID

Her *nuance!*

ELLA

YEAH!

DAVID

The undeniable *truth* she brings to the role!

ELLA

*(Dying laughing.)*

You're killing me—you're *killing* me!

DAVID

I mean any director worth his salt? Finds that kind of actress *repugnant.*

ELLA

I hope so. I *hope* so. . . .

DAVID

But Bertrand's an old *bag.* A has-been—a joke. A formerly-famous-now-completely-washed-up-*hack!*

ELLA

*(A bit shocked by his vitriol.)*

Dad . . .!

DAVID

*I* can't help it! *I* didn't make him that way!

ELLA

Okay, okay. . . .

DAVID

I knew he was a moron when I sent him my play—

ELLA

"Slow Burn"?

DAVID

No, an older draft of the new one—the one I'm working on now—

ELLA

"Canarsie?"

DAVID

That was a working title, it's untitled now—

ELLA

Oh.

DAVID

—and he didn't even read it. He sent a note to my *agent*. "I'm a great admirer of David's," he wrote, "But I'm afraid my calendar year is full."

*He laughs darkly.*

ELLA

Well . . .

DAVID

What.

ELLA

He *is* . . . really . . . busy. . . .

DAVID

Oh Jesus Christ, Ella—don't make me throw up.

ELLA

*(Suddenly reticent.)*
What . . .?

DAVID

He's not "busy." Ella! He's *afraid*.

ELLA

"Afraid?"

DAVID

He's *safe*.

ELLA

*(Not quite understanding.)*
"Safe". . .?

DAVID

He knows that at this stage in his sputtering, stagnant, *life*less career, the critics only *like* you if you're "safe."

ELLA

Okay.

DAVID

If you do the same bullshit they've been stroking your *dick* for for thirty years—just regurgitate the same *schlock* you've been spooning us for decades and dress it up like it's new when anyone with half a brain can clearly see it's *garbage*.

ELLA

Okay.

DAVID

*(With fiery resolve.)*
But that's the *one thing* you *never* want to be, Ella.

ELLA

Okay.

DAVID

Be trans*gressive*.

ELLA

Okay. . . .

DAVID

Be up*setting*.

ELLA

Okay . . .!

DAVID

Be *bewildering!*

ELLA

Okay!

DAVID

But above all—above *all else?* Do *not* be safe.
    *(Beat.)*
<u>Be anything but safe.</u>
        *She beams at him.*

ELLA

Thanks, Dad. *Thanks.*
        *He smiles back at her. Pours himself more wine.*

DAVID

So it makes *sense* he'd cast a trampy twig like "Clementine" in your
role.

ELLA

Right!

DAVID

Better cast a non-*threatening* Nina so all the men in the audience who
think they're *Konstantin* don't feel completely *emasculated!*

ELLA

*Right!*

DAVID

Plus, I'm sure he just wanted something *pretty* to look at in the rehearsal
room while he fades away into utter ob*scurity!*

ELLA

    *(Erupting in a fit of giggles.)*
Oh Dad—oh *Dad . . .!*

DAVID

And that's why he cast her and not you.
        *Beat.*

ELLA

    *(Stung.)*
Oh. . . .

DAVID

    *(With a shrug.)*
I'm not saying you're ugly. . . .

ELLA

*(On the verge of tears.)*
Thanks.

DAVID

I'm just saying you're *interesting*.

ELLA

*(Trying hard not to cry.)*
Okay. . . .

*Beat.*

DAVID

And a little ugly.

ELLA

*(Tears about to spill.)*
*Dad.* . . .

DAVID

It was a joke! Jesus! Can't you take a *joke?!*

ELLA

*(Brushing tears away.)*
Yeah. . . .

DAVID

*(Drags on cigarette.)*
You're never gonna get very far in this life if you don't have a sense
of humor about yourself.

ELLA

*(Glumly.)*
Okay. . . .

DAVID

*(Stubs out his cigarette.)*
You're brilliant, El. And if you seem like you have a brain? Then you're
a Masha, I guess. In his book, I mean. He has no imagination or
vision or *taste*.

ELLA

But . . .

DAVID

What.

ELLA

*(Reticent.)*
I . . . like . . . him. . . .

DAVID

*(Gravely.)*
Ella.

ELLA

What . . .?

DAVID

You "like" him?

ELLA

*(Mustering courage.)*
He's nice. . . .

DAVID

He's "nice?"

ELLA

He is! He's fun. He's smart. He's good.

DAVID

He's *"fun?"* He's *"smart?"* He's *"good?"*

ELLA

He . . . takes *care* of us.

DAVID

He *fucked* you, Ella!

ELLA

Dad!

DAVID

He *did!* He gave *her* your part!

ELLA

It wasn't . . . "my part". . . .

DAVID

Don't *say* that! It was. It *is*.

ELLA

Okay. Okay. . . .

DAVID

But now it's hers. And the real tragedy is—and you know this, right?
—that the critics fucking *cream* themselves over bimbos like that.

ELLA

*I know . . .!*

DAVID

And it's always the girl like that who gets the "love letter"—the *New
York Times* Stamp of Approval. . . .

ELLA

Oh god! It's so fucking—*arbitrary!* Who gets . . . annointed—

DAVID

—exactly!—

ELLA

—and who gets . . .

DAVID

Overlooked, I know! It's as random and meaningless as the Universe . . .

ELLA

*(Desperately sad.)*

Right. . . .

DAVID

With stakes as loaded and consequential as a game of Russian
Roulette.

ELLA

*(Near despair.)*

*Right . . .!*

*Beat.*

DAVID

*(Suddenly full of fire, again.)*

But there's an answer!

ELLA

*(Now hopeful.)*

There is?!

DAVID

Of course!

ELLA

*(Terribly relieved.)*
Oh good!

DAVID

It's God.

    *Beat.*

DAVID

Just kidding!

ELLA

Oh.

DAVID

It's *you.*

ELLA

Oh . . .?

DAVID

*You* have a *power*—a *control* that nobody else has—that *nobody* can take away from you.

ELLA

*(Getting excited again.)*
I do?

DAVID

We *all* do!

ELLA

Oh *wow . . .!*

DAVID

So you know what you gotta do?

ELLA

What?

DAVID

You know what you gotta say to them?

ELLA

What?!

DAVID

*Go fuck yourself.*

ELLA

Right!

DAVID

Go hang yourself on a noose and die.

ELLA

(Laughs.)
*Wow!*

DAVID

And then you've gotta say—you know what you've gotta say next?

ELLA

*What?!*

DAVID

You've gotta say what my old boss Milo Koppler always said—

ELLA

Oh god, *him.*

DAVID

Yes, "oh god, *him!*" He was a cocksucker, sure, but he taught me something I never forgot, and you shouldn't either—

ELLA

I know, I *know—*

DAVID

You know he was one of those spiritual, Zen-crazy, windbags—

ELLA

(Laughs.)
Like Trudie!

DAVID

(Chuckling.)
Exactly! Like your Aunt Trudie (the sanctimonious sow)—

ELLA

—hah!—

DAVID

But *brilliant.*

ELLA

Of course.

DAVID

A brilliant playwright, god oh god. . . .

ELLA

I know, I *know*—

DAVID

And my god, I couldn't *believe* I got that job! I mean, can you imagine? Me, a scrawny little knock-kneed Jewish boy from Sheepshead Bay, with acne and a s-s-s-st-stutter!

ELLA

*(Giggling.)*

Oh god . . .!

DAVID

The only job I'd ever had was in a *cat food factory!* Seventeen years old, a straight-D student, raised by a Russian widower who only wanted a son who would—

*(As his father; Russian accent.)*

—"make him proud"—

ELLA

*(Empathetic.)*

Oh, Dad. . . .

DAVID

*(As his father; Russian accent.)*

"A real American boy"—*(Dropping the accent.)*—who could play catch with his old man like the other kids on the block, and study hard and get good grades, and go to college! Be a *doctor,* be a *lawyer,* be a goddamn *dental hygienist,* just as long as he wasn't an *artist.*

ELLA

*(Heart breaking with compassion.)*

Oh, Daddy . . .! Oh, Dad. . . .

DAVID

*(As his father; Russian accent.)*

"Hey son, you want to throw ball around?"

*(Dropping accent.)*

My pops would ask, as if to *torment* me. And I'd try! Oh god did I try. But it's as if I had a magnetic energy that *repulsed* the ball—I'm telling you—it went *everywhere* except inside my mitt!

ELLA

Oh no! Oh *no* . . .*!*

DAVID

But Trudie! Oh, she could throw and catch like fucking Joe DiMaggio! I swear I knew she'd grow up to be a dyke, that's how good her arm was.

ELLA

Dad. . . .

DAVID

*(As his father; Russian accent.)*

"I wish you mother could be alive today, to see the beautiful woman you sister has become."

*(Dropping the accent.)*

Of course she wasn't beautiful—she looked like fucking Karl Malden in a dress—

ELLA

*(Giggling naughtily.)*

Dad . . .!

DAVID

She did! I bet she *still* does!

ELLA

Okay. . . .

DAVID

But at least she—

*(Russian accent.)*

"*made him proud.*"

*(Dropping the accent.)*

*Studied hard, president of the debate team, editor of the high school newspaper. . . .*

ELLA

Right—*right.*

DAVID

(Little did he know at the time that she was a closeted commie and a pothead!)

ELLA

Right—surprise!

DAVID

And my little sister Dopie—just as sweet as could be: never talked back, did her homework like a good girl, more friends than any kid you ever saw. . . .

ELLA

Awww . . . *Dopie* . . .!

DAVID

(A smile crossing his face as he fondly remembers.)

She used to dance around the house like Shirley Temple!

(Sings.)

"Animal crackers in my soup. . . ."

(Laughs.)

Drove us crazy . . .!

(Remembers.)

The sweetest thing. . . . No matter how shitty things got—when our mother died, when our pops whipped off his belt, and. . . .

(Beat; he remembers.)

She always had a smile, and a hug, and a. . . .

Beat. He goes into a memory.

ELLA

Dad . . .?

DAVID

(Coming back to the present with a surge of energy.)

And then there was me. Hah! Your famous dad: an antisocial, asthmatic *hermit* who had a panic attack every time he opened a *textbook* and spent all his time under the covers with a flashlight, reading *plays!*

ELLA

(With real affection.)

Yes! Yes . . .!

DAVID

But you know how I got through it all?

                            ELLA
How?

                            DAVID
You wanna know my secret?

                            ELLA
I *do!*

                            DAVID
Well not a lot of people have the balls to say this, but I've always
said it—I said it in my memoirs and I said it in that thing I wrote for
*The New Yorker* (which they butchered, but still), and I said it to
Charlie Rose, and I'll say it to you, now—

                            ELLA
Thanks, Dad!

                            DAVID
<u>I always knew I was gonna be famous</u>.

        *Beat.*


                            ELLA
        *(Blown away.)*
Wow.

                            DAVID
Seventeen years old, no friends—my only friend was my kid sister!—

                            ELLA
Right!

                            DAVID
—and I'd read her scenes from my plays—and Dopie was only a *kid*
(six, seven years old), but I could tell from the look on her face: my
stuff was *good*. It was better than good. It was *brilliant!*

                            ELLA
It was—it *is!*

                            DAVID
And that's all you need—*one fan*. It can be your goddamn *kid sister!*
You just need one voice—*one voice*—that's not in your own head—
one person who says: You're it. You're a genius. *You're gonna be a
star.*

ELLA

*Right. . . .*

DAVID

And that's what I am for you, kid.

ELLA

Thanks, Dad. Thanks!

DAVID

Don't ever forget it.

ELLA

I won't!

DAVID

I mean you're lucky, girlie—you got exposed to what you love so young.

ELLA

I *know.*

DAVID

So many poor fuckers never *find* that thing that turns them on—that makes them *tick*, that makes the *hell* we have to endure every day somehow—hilariously, insanely, senselessly!—somehow *worth* _it_.

ELLA

It's *true.*

DAVID

And boy was I lucky I grew up in the fifties, chickie! I mean the theater wasn't just for blue-haired ladies with hearing aids back then!

ELLA

Right!

DAVID

When I was a kid, a ticket to a Broadway show was—well guess: how much do you think it cost to go see Mary Martin play "Peter Pan?"
>    *(Sings.)*
"*I'm flying . . . !*"

ELLA

How much? How much?!

DAVID

The first Broadway production of "Waiting for Godot" with Bert Lahr as Estragon?

*(Doing Bert Lahr as Estragon.)*
*"Nothing to be done."*

ELLA

How *much*? How *much*?!

DAVID

The *original production* of "West Side Story," with lyrics by an
unknown Jewish kid from the Upper West Side named Stephen
Sondheim, at the Winter Garden theater, 1957?
*(Sings.)*
*"When you're a jet you're a jet!"*

ELLA

*(Sings.)*
*"Stick to your own kiiind . . . ."*

DAVID

*(Sings, devoutly.)*
*"There's a place . . . for us . . ."*

ELLA

*(Sings, nearly weeping.)*
*"Someday . . . Somewhere . . . !"*

DAVID

It cost *six dollars.*

ELLA

*(Utter disbelief.)*
No.

DAVID

For the *best seat.*

ELLA

NO.

DAVID

You can't imagine it, can you? Every Wednesday I'd skip out of school
after third period, take my wages from the cat food factory, hop on
the BMT Sea Beach Line, get off at Times Square Forty-Second
Street, and buy a ticket to a matinee of any show I liked. That was
my food, my friendships, my romance, my *joy.*

ELLA

*(Enamored.)*

*Wow . . .!*

DAVID

And what a horror—can you imagine?!—to return on Thursday to the drudgery and *hell* of my quotidian toil.

ELLA

Of *course!*

DAVID

*(Back into his story.)*

Well, I come home one night from the cat food factory and my father's there, sitting in the dark, a candle burning, and . . .

*(Portentously—enjoying the spinning of this yarn.)*

I know something's up.

ELLA

*(Enjoying the spectacle also.)*

Oh no. Oh *no . . . .*

DAVID

*(As his father, Russian accent—cold and severe.)*

"David, you listening?"

*(As his stuttering adolescent self:)*

"S-s-s-ure," I say—*(As his father, Russian accent.)* "You better sit down," my pops says, real quiet—I'll never forget it—and I sit, and he says, solemn as if someone's had a fucking heart attack: "David, you principal of you school called. He say you been skipping class and doing god knows what"—it's true, I was like Laura in the goddamn "Glass Menagerie," playing hooky on my typing classes 'cause I just wanted to play with my glass *figurines,* goddammit!

ELLA

*(Gleefully.)*

Goddammit! *Godammit!*

DAVID

*(As his father, Russian accent.)*

"David, you have you head up you ass with you *plays,* with you theater, with you *writing.* And now you being kicked out of school."

ELLA

*(Delighted.)*

Oh god . . .!

DAVID

And you know what he said next?

ELLA

What. What?!

DAVID

"And now . . . *I kicking you out too.*"

ELLA

*(Really sad.)*

Oh no!

DAVID

And you know what I did? You know what your silly old dad did?

ELLA

What. *What?!*

DAVID

I didn't say a *word*—I just went into my room, I grabbed my knapsack
and I just started throwing shit in it—Dopie screaming "Davey! *Davey!*
Don't go! Don't *go-o-o-o-o-o!*"

ELLA

*(Heart breaking.)*

Oh my *god* . . .!

DAVID

And Trudie doing god knows what in the other room—probably smoking grass and playing with herself while reading *Das Kapital*—

ELLA

—hah! What a witch—

DAVID

And I jammed a few clothes and a toothbrush in my knapsack and
you know the *one* other thing I brought?

ELLA

*(Enraptured.)*

What. *What?*

DAVID

A *book*. My favorite book. A *play*. A play I'd read maybe forty, fifty times: my worn, mint-green, Samuel French edition of "My Brother Joe."

ELLA

*(Deeply moved.)*

Oh . . . *god* . . . !

DAVID

By *Milo fucking Koppler.* And I *split.* And Dopie chasing me down the street as I stormed toward the subway—"Davey! *Davey!*" And I *shoved* her off me—"Get *AWAY from me!*" I screamed . . .

*(Beat; he remembers.)*

I'll never forget it. . . .

> *Suddenly he seems as if he is about to cry. He is lost in thought, remembering.*

ELLA

*(Concerned.)*

Dad . . . ?

DAVID

*(Bouncing back.)*

And I got off the train at Times Square Forty-Second Street—I didn't know why! Except where else was I to go? I had *nowhere to go*—not a friend in the goddamn world. My only friends were—you know who my friends were?

ELLA

Who? Who?!

DAVID

Comden and Green. Irving Berlin. Rodgers and Hammerstein.

ELLA

*(Enthralled.)*

Yes. Yes!

DAVID

Chekhov! Shakespeare! Ibsen!

ELLA

Tennessee Williams!

DAVID

Eh, a bit of a lightweight, but sure.

ELLA

Thornton Wilder?

DAVID

Hit or miss, but often fun.

ELLA

*(Great idea.)*
Clifford Odets!

DAVID

YES. And more than any of 'em? *Milo Koppler.* 'Cause here was a guy like *me*: came from nothing, raised in Queens by immigrant idiots who didn't understand him and threw him out on his ass (in his case it's 'cause he was a fairy, but still)—

ELLA

—Dad—

DAVID

—don't *interrupt* me! Still! The point is: he *survived.*

ELLA

Right. Right!

DAVID

He *survived*, and then he went on to use that shit—to *use* all that *shit* from his miserable life and craft the most *perfect plays* of the twentieth century!

ELLA

Yes. *Yes!*

DAVID

I'll never forget it. . . .

ELLA

What?

DAVID

The first time I saw "My Brother Joe."

ELLA

Ohhh . . .!

DAVID

I was fourteen years old. Had just finished reading "Death of a
Salesman" for the very first time (I had to go to the fucking Columbus
Circle library to get a copy because you bet your ass there wasn't
one in all of Sheepshead Bay . . .!)

ELLA

Hah! Right!

DAVID

And I thought—oh Ella, of *course* I thought—this guy, this Arthur
Miller—this guy is *it*. You know? This *play* is—

ELLA
*(Rapturous.)*
I *know*. . . .

DAVID

Don't interrupt me!

ELLA
*(Under her breath.)*
—sorry—

DAVID

This *play* is . . . *everything* . . . I could want a play to be. This Willy is
. . . *my pops* . . .! This poor Linda is . . . my long-suffering ma. And
this brother! Biff! This is *my sister* . . .! Trudie!

ELLA

Right!

DAVID
(Conveniently she *looks* like a man, so there was no stretch there.)

ELLA
*(Giggling.)*
Right . . .!

DAVID
And this sad, sad . . . Happy. . . . That was me.
*(Beat.)*
That was me. . . .

ELLA

*(In heaven; near tears.)*

*Right.* . . .

*A beat. David reflects. Then—*

DAVID

But *then—*

ELLA

But then?

DAVID

I saw "My Brother Joe."

ELLA

Yes?

DAVID

And I knew.

ELLA

You knew?

DAVID

Arthur Miller was a hack.

ELLA

*(Incredulous.)*

Dad . . .!

DAVID

Okay, not a *hack*, but Ella, come *on!* When you read "Death of a Salesman" and you read "My Brother Joe," the truth is so clear it's like a *joke!*

ELLA

A—joke . . .?

DAVID

Willy Loman can't hold a candle to Joe Brodzinski!

ELLA

Right.

DAVID

Even the *language* Miller uses—"Attention must be *paid?*" Who *talks* like that?!

ELLA

Right!

DAVID

Just say—"Pay attention"!

ELLA

*Right!*

DAVID

"Nobody dast blame this man."

ELLA

What's that?

DAVID

That's a *line!* From the *play!*

ELLA

(*Incredulous.*)
From "Death of a *Salesman*" . . .?

DAVID

(*Nods.*)
In the requiem speech, Charley says about Willy: "Nobody *dast*
blame this man."

ELLA

That's . . . *terrible*. . . .

DAVID

I know! And nobody talks about it. Nobody says: "*Humans don't talk
this way . . .!*"

ELLA

(*Giggling.*)
Right. . . .

DAVID

I mean if your goal is to put *me*—to put *us*—on a stage? Then *write
like we talk.*

ELLA

Right . . .!

DAVID

Have your characters talk like *humans!* Like humans *speak.* In the
*world!*

ELLA

*Right!*

DAVID

And that's what Koppler did. I'll never forget it. The curtain came up on the first act of "My Brother Joe" and as soon as Adrian said that famous line:

DAVID                                      ELLA

"Did you turn the heat up?"      "Did you turn the heat up?"

DAVID

*Exactly.* I *knew:* This *is me.*

> *(Beat; reflects.)*

This . . . *is me.*

> *A beat.* DAVID *goes into a memory.*

DAVID

I saw that play sixteen times. . . .

> *A beat.*

ELLA

Dad . . .?

DAVID

> *(Bouncing back.)*

So you know what I did? You know what your silly old dad did?

ELLA

> *(On the edge of her seat.)*

What?

DAVID

A terrified seventeen-year-old boy alone in the world in the middle of Times Square at ten-thirty at night, with only a knapsack full of rags to my name?

ELLA

What?!

DAVID

I found a phone booth and I picked up the phone book—

ELLA

*(Loving this story.)*
—oh no, oh *no!*—

DAVID

—oh yes, oh *yes!*—and not even *conscious* of what I was doing, I flipped to the letter *K*, and—holy shit—*there he was!*

ELLA

*No!*

DAVID

*(As his seventeen-year-old self.)*
"H-h-h-h-hello, is this the office of the g-g-g-g-great American dramatist Milo K-k-k-k-Koppler?"

ELLA

Oh *god!*

DAVID

*(As Koppler; Queens accent.)*
"This ain't his office, it's his *home!* And you're waking him up!"

ELLA

*(Delighted.)*
Oh *NO!*

DAVID

*(Equally delighted.)*
Oh *YES!*
*(Knock-kneed adolescent David again:)*
"Um, w-w-w-w-well my name is David Bergenstein" (this was before I changed my name)—

ELLA

—right, right—

DAVID

—and then I heard myself say something—(to this day, I don't know why I said it—I swear it's as if someone *else* said it!)—I said "My name is David Bergenstein, and—

| DAVID | ELLA |
|---|---|
| "I am your successor." | "I am your succesor," right. |

*Beat.*

DAVID

Oh, you know this story?

ELLA

What? No.

DAVID

I've told it before?

ELLA

*(Starting to panic.)*
Maybe once or twice—maybe I read it in an interview somewhere.
Keep telling it—keep *telling* it! I love it. I *love* it . . .!

*He gets up to empty the ashtray.*

DAVID

*(Cold.)*
I won't bore you.

*He bangs the ashtray against the trash can to empty it.*

ELLA

*(Desperate.)*
No—no, tell it, *tell* it! You *have* to, Dad! I *love* your stories . . .!

*She pours him another glass of wine.*

*He looks at the glass. A beat. Then—*

*He returns to the table with the ashtray.*

ELLA

*(Terribly relieved.)*
Here. Here. . . .

*She hands him the glass. He takes a big sip.*

*He lights a new cigarette.*

DAVID

So: it turns out, Koppler tells me—my *idol* tells me!—that the *next*
*day* he's going into rehearsals for his new Broadway show—

ELLA

—oh god!—

DAVID

—and he tells me that it must be a "Higher Power" that I'm calling, because *he needs an assistant!*

ELLA

No. NO!

DAVID

Yes. YES!
   *(As Koppler.)*
"Will ya work for nothing?"
   *(As adolescent David.)*
"Of-of-of course I will!" I stammer, "B-b-b-but—"
   *(As Koppler.)*
"Spit it out, boy!"
   *(Adolescent David; pathetic, almost in tears.)*
"I-I-I-I-I have nowhere to s-s-s-s-s-*staaaaaay . . .!*"

ELLA

   *(Rapt.)*
You. Did. *Not*.

DAVID

I kid you not, girlie, your old man started *bawling* on the phone with this—this *god!*

ELLA

   *(Loving this.)*
Oh my *god!*

DAVID

There I was—a deflated balloon of a boy, crying my little eyes out on the corner of Forty-Eighth and Broadway like a colicky toddler with diaper rash.

ELLA

Jesus. Christ.

DAVID

You said it! Jesus CHRIST! And you know what he said (the old queen)?

ELLA

(Dad!)

DAVID

(What!? He was an old queen!) He said, "Take the train to West Fourth Street, and I'll meet you there."

ELLA

*Wow.*

DAVID

And when I climbed up those stairs, out of the subway—like fucking *Orpheus* ascending from the jaws of Hades, there he was—Marlon Brando meets Ernest Hemingway (I mean, who knew a nancy could look like such a matinee idol!)—

ELLA

*(Under her breath.)*

—Dad!—

DAVID

*(Ignoring her.)*

—my idol, my hero, my savior: Milo Koppler, in the flesh.

*A beat. Then—*

ELLA

Wow. *Wow.* . . .

DAVID

And then he took me back to his place and he raped me.

ELLA

Dad!

DAVID

Just kidding! But that was the beginning—right away he offers me a cigarette, and I think: "This guy—this guy I could get to like!"

ELLA

Right!

DAVID

And we smoke and we walk and we talk—I never met a man so curious, it was like the fucking Spanish Inquisition, all the questions that fairy asked me!

ELLA

—Dad—

DAVID

And we get back to his place, and I'm telling you, El, this apartment was unlike anything I'd ever seen—I mean I had no idea people *lived* like this! In *New York City!* A *duplex* on MacDougal Street with exposed brick and high ceilings and an *eat-in kitchen.* An <u>*eat-in kitchen!*</u> I thought, "This guy's got it made! He can *eat* in his own *kitchen!*"

ELLA
*(Laughs.)*
Right!

DAVID
*(Gesturing around him.)*
And look at me now!

ELLA
*Right!*

DAVID
We can eat in here all day long!

ELLA
*(Giggling.)*
*Right* . . .!

DAVID
And I'm looking around this—this *palace,* and I say, "Is your wife at home?"

ELLA
Hah!

DAVID
I mean *I* didn't know! I didn't know *anything* about this guy, of course —except that he'd written the most perfect play I could ever *imagine*—and . . . you know, such a big apartment, I just *assumed.* . . .

ELLA
Of course!

DAVID
And he looked at me. And he took a beat. And then he said: "I'm not married."

ELLA
Wow. . . .

DAVID
And Ella—oh my god. The way he said it. I just knew.

ELLA

You knew . . .?

DAVID

I knew. *He was Joe.*

ELLA

Ohhh. . . .

DAVID

In his *youth,* I mean. This tragic, brilliant . . . *tortured* queer who could *pass* as straight but who knew . . . who *knew* . . . he was a walking lie.

ELLA

Oh god. Oh *god.* . . .

DAVID

And *then* I think: "Jesus! I hope he doesn't make a *pass* at me . . .!"

ELLA

(*Giggling.*)

Right . . .!

DAVID

But he doesn't, of course. He just says (so polite): "You want anything to drink?" And I say, "Well sure! I'll take a Scotch on the rocks." And he says (the old bastard), "I don't keep alcohol in the house." Well this I couldn't believe. "Why not?!" I ask. "I don't drink anymore," he says."I've been sober for eleven years." Well of course I have no fucking clue what he's talking about, but I don't say anything— I just let him pour me a seltzer, plop a wedge of lime in there and make one for himself, and I think, "This guy. . . this guy is *weird!*"

ELLA

*Yeah!*

DAVID

And the next day he brings me to the first rehearsal for his new Broadway show, "Pigs and Promises."

ELLA

Oh my god, *that* was "Pigs and Promises"?!

DAVID

(*Grinning.*)

It sure was, and just like that—like *fate* had *ordained* it—I became his roommate, his protégé, his assistant.

ELLA

Jesus Christ.

DAVID

*And* his lover.

ELLA

Dad!

DAVID

Just kidding! Anyway, the next few weeks are a *blur*—my job is to
sit next to my hero and just absorb—*absorb* . . .! Occasionally I'm
getting him a coffee or running out for some smokes, but mostly I'm
just sitting there *agog*—

ELLA

—oh *god*—

DAVID

—and when we're not rehearsing we're staying up late, smoking
and laughing and not *drinking*, okay, but just talking—*talking* about the
play. *Talking about his play!* This genius, asking me what *I* think about
this line, what *I* think about this scene, *what I think . . .!*
      *(Laughs.)*
And I let him know! I give him *suggestions!* And he *takes* 'em . . .!

ELLA

      *(Nearly swooning.)*
Oh wow . . .!

DAVID

I *know!* And the whole thing's a dream, of course . . .
      *(Beat.)*
But there's a problem.

ELLA

      *(On the edge of her seat.)*
Oh no.

DAVID

      *(Nods, darkly.)*
There's this one guy in the cast who's a fucking *pest*—

ELLA

Oh *no!*

DAVID

The guy playing Uncle Seymour—

ELLA

—that's a great part!—

DAVID—

I know! And he's this over-the-hill, tubby little *character* actor named
Sidney Crumm, and this numbnut's always saying things like:
"Koppler, my character wouldn't *say* that, Koppler what *motivates*
this? Koppler, I don't buy these *given circumstances*," fucking bullshit
faggoty drama queen crap—

ELLA

Dad. . . .

DAVID

What?! He was acting like a fucking faggot!

ELLA

Okay. . . .

DAVID

You kids are so fucking *precious* with your language, today! You
need to lighten up—

ELLA

*Okay.*

DAVID

Calling someone a faggot doesn't mean they're a *faggot*—it means
they're *acting* like a faggot.

ELLA

Okay. . . .

DAVID

So we tell this fucking faggot we're *not* changing the text—the text is
the *text*.

ELLA

Right.

DAVID

So now it's Opening Night, and this is back when the critics all *came*
Opening Night—

ELLA

—oh *god*-

DAVID

—and me and Koppler, we can't *sit!* I'd never *seen* the guy so
keyed up . . .! We're standing in the back of the Lunt-Fontanne,
sweat pouring down our mugs like we're both about to get *fucked*
for the very first time!

ELLA

Of *course!*

DAVID

And the show's going *great*—I mean, like a *song!* It *hums*, it *purrs*,
it *slides* with effortless elegance like a fucking Rolls *Royce* on an
empty road . . .!

ELLA

(*Entranced.*)

Wow . . .!

DAVID

And me and Koppler, we're not even *breathing*—we're just *in it*,
you know—both of us, together—just watching and listening and
thinking—"*Please, please, let this last! Please let this never stop!
Please let them like it! Please, oh please . . .!*"

ELLA

Oh god, oh *god* . . .!

DAVID

And the curtain's about to go down at the end of Act One, and right
before it does, Uncle Seymour has that monologue (you know the
one), about his sister and her baby? And the stillbirth, and how he
ran away?

ELLA

Of *course.*

DAVID

And Sidney Crumm launches into that monologue—I mean this
beautiful, *flawlessly* crafted, fucking *wrenching* monologue (which
would turn out to be one of the most famous soliloquies of the
twentieth century)—

ELLA

—I *know!*—

DAVID

—and Crumm falls to his knees, and he mops his brow, lifts his
stubby little arms to the heavens—

ELLA

—oh *no*—

DAVID

—and me and Koppler turn to each other, chills running down our spines, our extremities *tingling*, the blood *draining* from our faces, because of course we're both thinking the same thing—

ELLA

*(Delighted.)*
—oh *no!*—

DAVID

"*That wasn't in the blocking.*"

ELLA

OH. NO!

DAVID

. . . and the *son-of-a-bitch* launches into an *improvised monologue* that he fucking *rips* out of his own pathetic, smarmy, *hairy asshole* that goes on for—I kid you not—*seven minutes.*

ELLA

*(A bloodcurdling scream.)*
AAAAAAAAAHHHHHHHHH!

DAVID

And of course there is *nothing we can do!* We are just . . . powerless. *Powerless!* All we can do is stand there and watch as the nightmare unfolds, and feel our souls freeze over and just die—just *die!*—inside.

ELLA

*(Deeply empathetic.)*
Of *course!*

DAVID

I mean, this play that I knew inside and out—this play that was *sacred* to me! This play that I *worshipped!* This play that was my. . . .
    *(Beat; reflects.)*
And this fucking hack just *mutilates* it in front of my eyes . . .!

ELLA

*(With deep empathy.)*
I *know . . .!*

DAVID

I felt like fucking *Abraham*, blindly leading his only son to slaughter . . .!
*Raskolnikov,* rotting to death in a Siberian prison in pointless atone-
ment . . .! Or *Hamlet!* Accepting the poisoned tip of his best friend's
blade into his soft, defenseless guts . . .! "*This is the end,*" I thought,
"*this is it: how it all falls apart.*"

ELLA

*(Softly.)*
Oh. . . god. . . .

*A beat. He remembers.* ELLA *watches him, pained.*

DAVID

*(Shaking his head; muttering, almost to himself . . . )*
"Nothing to be done. . . . Nothing to . . . be . . . done. . . ."

*A beat. Then—*

DAVID

*(Back to* ELLA.*)*
And the curtain falls and I turn to my boss, the great Milo Koppler—
I mean I can barely *speak,* I'm so boiled up—and I say: "Boss, I'm
gonna fucking knock his *lights* out, I swear to god—" I mean all
ninety pounds of me, right?—but I *would,* you know? For this guy.
For this *play. . . .*

ELLA

Of *course . . .!*

DAVID

And Koppler turns to me, and I see, suddenly . . . he's not sweating
anymore. . . . He looks almost calm—tranquil even, almost . . . *serene.*
. . . His eyes have a—a *stillness.* He almost seems like he's . . . *smiling.*

ELLA

*(Bewildered.)*
What . . .?

DAVID

And he says to me, you know what he says? "Ya know what, son?
Ya know what we gotta do?"

ELLA

*(Enraptured.)*
What . . .?!

DAVID

"*Pray for him.*"

ELLA

(*Baffled.*)
What?!?

DAVID

"He's sick," Koppler says. "He's suffering. He's in pain. *Let's pray for him*. He deserves our prayers."

*Beat.* ELLA *is agape.*

DAVID

And with that he turns around and walks away, out the door of the theater and down the block toward Sardi's. I don't even know if he watched the second act!

ELLA

. . . what the . . .? *What . . .?*

DAVID

I know.

ELLA

Why?

DAVID

I *know!* I stood there dumbfounded—how could he be so *blasé?!* This was his *baby!*

ELLA

Right!

DAVID

How could he not stand up and *fight* for it?! Go backstage and knock that guy *around!* Give him a piece of his *mind!* Make him *pay*—make him *pay!*

ELLA

I know! I *know!*

DAVID

And then a thought crossed my mind—you know what I thought?

ELLA

(*Hanging on his every word.*)
What. *What?*

DAVID

I thought, "You know what, Koppler? You're right, buddy. I *am* gonna pray for him. And you know what else? You know what I'm gonna do next? I'm gonna get on my fucking knees, and I'm gonna pray for you, you traitor. I'm gonna pray for you so hard I'm gonna make my *knees bleed.* That's what I'm gonna do for *you,* you dickless pussy."

ELLA

Oh wow . . .*!*

DAVID

*(A growl.)*

And I left the theater and I walked all the way to MacDougal Street and I packed up my stuff and I *split.* And I never saw that cocksucker ever again.

ELLA

Oh *god . . .!*

DAVID

*(Bringing it all home.)*

And *that's* what you've gotta say to these fucking critics, Ella! "You're gonna be number one in my prayers tonight, buddy!" *That's* what you've gotta say—because you've got to *pity* them—

ELLA

*(It's all sinking in.)*

Ohhhh. . . .

DAVID

Pine for them. Weep for them. *Pray* for them.

ELLA

Right.

DAVID

Because you know what they are?

ELLA

*What?*

DAVID

They're sick. Like Koppler said—"Sick. Suffering. Pray for them."

ELLA

*(Pensive.)*

Right. . . .

DAVID

And *then* kick 'em in the balls and tell them to go fuck themselves!

ELLA

*(Laughing.)*
Right—*right!*

DAVID

He didn't mean it like that, of course, but that's what I made of it, and that's what I've done my *whole life*—my *whole career*—that's how I've made a *name* for myself—

ELLA

How? *How?*

DAVID

<u>I take the bullshit people feed me and I make it my own.</u>

ELLA

*(Deeply struck.)*
Wow.

*(Blown away.)*
*Wow.*

*He extinguishes his cigarette. Takes a cigarette out of his pack.*

*She goes for her pack, sees it's empty.*

ELLA

Oh.

DAVID

What.

ELLA

I'm all out.

DAVID

Oh.

ELLA

Can I have. . . one of yours . . . ?

*Beat.*

DAVID

I've only got one left.

ELLA

Oh.

DAVID

Sorry.

ELLA

It's cool.

DAVID

Uch—I hate how you kids say, "It's cool. . . ."

*He lights his cigarette. He suddenly seems very drunk.*

DAVID

As if I thought it *wouldn't* be fucking cool! Hah. You've gotta learn to use *language* better, or you're never gonna be a good writer.

ELLA

I'm not a writer. . . .

DAVID

*(Erupting.)*

Don't *SAY* that! Goddammit. You're a *great* writer! You've just gotta *write* some shit.

ELLA

Okay. . . .

*He smokes. She drinks some wine.*

*A beat. Then—*

ELLA

*(Delicately.)*

Trudie's a writer. . . right . . .?

*Beat.*

DAVID

I guess.

*Beat.*

ELLA

Have you read her—

DAVID

Who cares.

*Beat.*

ELLA

When was the last time—

DAVID

Who *cares*.

*A beat. Then—*

ELLA
*(Plucking up some courage.)*
Dad . . .?

DAVID

What.

ELLA

Did you ever. . . regret it . . .?

DAVID

What?

ELLA

Walking out . . .?

DAVID

*What?*

ELLA
*(Mustering more courage.)*
Did you regret . . . leaving Koppler?

*(Beat.)*

Since the show turned out to be. . . such a hit . . .?

*He stares at her, his eyes glassy. For a moment it seems
as if he possibly hasn't heard her. . .*

*A beat. Then—*

DAVID

What kind of a fucking question is that?

ELLA
*(Scared.)*
I—I'm sorry.

DAVID

Does it *look* like I'm suffering now?

ELLA

. . . no . . .?

DAVID

Does it *look* like I have any goddamn *"regrets?!"*

ELLA

No . . .!

DAVID

You think I *"regret"* walking out of my father's house at seventeen?
Escaping his abuse? You think I lie awake at night *crying* about it?
*"Boo hoo hoo!"*? How I never saw him again, piece of *shit* that he
was?! How I mailed back his letters—every one of them—unopened?!
You think I'm *pining* over that epic mis*take?*

ELLA

*(Near tears.)*

N-no. . . .

DAVID

And Dopie? You think I *"regret"* leaving her? You think I *knew* when I
walked out—when I told her to get lost on the corner of Coney Island
Ave and Avenue Z—you think I *knew* that six months later, she'd get
hit by a fucking B21 bus because my father was too *hung over* to
take her to school?! You think I fucking *planned* all that?!

ELLA

Of course not! *No!*

DAVID

You think I "regret" telling *Trudie to go fuck herself?* After she blamed
*Dopie's death on me?!* After she wrote a fucking *book about it?!*
About *me?!?* You think I *"regret"* keeping that *cunt* out of my life?!
And yours?!?

ELLA

No, Dad. *No!*

DAVID

*(Venomous.)*

*Every* thing I did—*every* decision I made—led me *right here—right to
this moment,* here with you. You think I *"regret"* having *you?*

ELLA

*(Nearly crying; terrified.)*

I—I don't kn-o-o-ow . . .!

DAVID

I *regret nothing.* Do you know why?

*(Grabs her chin; spitting the words.)*
*Do you know why?*

ELLA

*(Crying.)*
N-no . . .!

DAVID

*(Yanking her head by the chin.)*
Because *it gave me my play.*

*(Lets go of her chin.)*
If I hadn't done all that—if none of that *shit* had ever happened?
I never would've written "The Battle of Long Island." I never would've
won the *Pulitzer,* two *Tony's* . . .! I never would've gone on to write
"Gavalt!" Or "Mr. Feingold!!" Or "Four Questions!!!" Goddammit,
I never would've gotten a fucking *Academy Award*—

ELLA

*(Under her breath.)*
—nomination.

*Beat.*

DAVID

What.

*Beat.*

ELLA

"Nomination," I said—the Academy Award. . . *nomination*—I'm agree-
ing with you. . . .

*He stares at her.*

*A beat. Then—*

DAVID

All right, fine. "Nomination." Jesus.

*Beat.*

*He gets up to empty the ashtray.*

DAVID

What are you, a fucking *fact checker?*

*Beat.*

ELLA

*(Softly.)*
I'm sorry.

DAVID

Smartass.

ELLA

I'm sorry . . .!

DAVID

Forget it.

> *Beat.*

ELLA

> *(Trying not to cry.)*

You *should've* won . . .!

> *Beat.*

DAVID

> *(Icy.)*

"It's cool."

> *He BANGS the ashtray, hard, several times against the trash can, to empty it. He keeps BANGING it, aggressively, long after he needs to.*
>
> *He stops.*
>
> *A beat.*
>
> *He stands there, hunched over the trash, panting.*
>
> ELLA *tries not to cry.*

ELLA

Dad? I'm sorry. I'm sorry, Dad. I'm sorry. . . .

> DAVID *stands there; says nothing.*

ELLA

Come on Dad, have one more glass of wine with me.

> *She pours him another glass of wine and holds it out to him.*

ELLA

Come on, Dad—*please* . . .!

> *He looks at her.*
>
> *A beat. Then—*

DAVID

I think you've had enough to drink.

> *Beat.*

ELLA

What?

                              DAVID
You get nasty when you're drunk.

                              ELLA
        *(Bewildered.)*
I do . . .?

                              DAVID
You need to learn how to hold your liquor.

                              ELLA
Okay.

                              DAVID
You've gotta do what I do. Set your limit—three drinks. And then
have maybe one or two more. And that's it.

                              ELLA
Okay. . . .

        DAVID *gets up.*

                              DAVID
You wanna be an adult? You've gotta drink like an adult.

                              ELLA
*Okay . . .!*

        DAVID *crosses to a cupboard.*

                              DAVID
You've gotta know when it's time to stop.

        DAVID *opens the cupboard and retrieves a small bong.
        Carries it over to the table. Sits down.*

        *He lights it. He inhales. He holds the pot in his lungs.*

        *A beat. Then—he exhales.*

                              DAVID
Oh yeah. Oh yeah. . . .

                              ELLA
Can I have a hit?

                              DAVID
If you say you're sorry.

                              ELLA
I'm sorry.

        *He takes another hit.*

DAVID

Say it like you mean it.

ELLA

I'm sorry. I'm *sorry . . .!*

> *He takes another hit.*

DAVID

Eh, I'm not buying it. . . .

ELLA

I'm sorry, Dad—I'm *sorry . . .!* Please, Dad—*please . . .!*

> *He hands her the bong.*

DAVID

Don't get too stoned.

ELLA

Thank you. *Thank* you . . .!

> *She lights the bong and inhales.*
>
> *A beat. Then—she exhales.*

DAVID

You've gotta hold it in longer.

ELLA

I know. I *know.*

> *They pass the bong back and forth, and smoke, in silence.*
>
> *A beat. Then—*

DAVID

You're my little dumpling. You know that, right?

> ELLA *starts to cry.*

DAVID

Ohhh. . . .

> ELLA *cries.*

DAVID

Ella. . . .

> ELLA *cries.*

DAVID

Ella . . .!

ELLA

> *(Crying, hard.)*

I love you, Dad.

DAVID

Come here.

> DAVID *pats his lap.* ELLA *gets up and sits on his lap. He rocks her. He kisses her head.*

DAVID

You remember the game we used to play when you were little . . .?
When you would get out of the bathtub . . .?

> ELLA *smiles through her tears.*

ELLA

Turtle. . . .

DAVID

*(Deeply affectionate, stroking her hair.)*
That's right. Turtle . . .! You would be all tiny and naked and wet, and
I would wrap you in a towel and throw you on the bed and roll you
around! And you'd pretend to be a turtle inside your shell. . . .

> ELLA *cries and laughs.*

DAVID

"Where's my turtle?!" I'd say. "I can't find her!

> *He tickles her. She giggles.*

| DAVID | ELLA |
|---|---|
| "She's hiding in her shell . . .!" | "She's hiding in her shell . . .!" |

> *He tickles her. She squirms, and laughs through her tears.*

DAVID

You loved that game.

> *Beat. She beams at him.*

ELLA

I love you so much.

> DAVID'*s eyes mist over. He strokes her hair.*

DAVID

My baby. My baby. . . .

ELLA

I don't want you to die. Ever.

DAVID

I'm not going to. I never will.

ELLA

*(Very scared, suddenly.)*
I can't live without you . . .!

DAVID

*(Stroking her hair.)*
Well, that's the beauty of being famous, Ella. You get to live forever!

ELLA

I'm trying. I'm *trying . . .!*
*Beat.*

DAVID

Get off.

ELLA

What?

DAVID

Get off my lap. My leg's falling asleep.

ELLA

Oh. Sorry.

ELLA *gets off his lap. She sits back down in her chair.* DAVID *puts out his cigarette.*

*A beat. Then—*

DAVID

Do you think it's time? Do you think it's *time . . .?*

ELLA

Oh! I don't know. . . .

DAVID

*(Sing-song.)*
I think it's time. I think it's *tiiiiime. . . .!*

ELLA

I'm *scared . . .!*

DAVID

I know, I know. Just remember: they're sick and suffering.

ELLA

*(Apprehensive.)*

Okay.

DAVID

Pray for them.

ELLA

*(Very nervous.)*

Okay.

DAVID

Give me your phone.

ELLA

*(Terrified.)*

Okay. . . .

ELLA *reaches into her pocket and pulls out her iPhone. She hands it to* DAVID.

*He presses a button.*

DAVID

You have to un*lock* it!

ELLA

Sorry.

*He hands her back the phone. She types something in. Hands it back to him.*

*He types something into the phone.*

DAVID

It's loading. It's loading. . . .

ELLA

*(Dying with anticipation.)*

Oh god. . . .

DAVID

Do you know who it was?

ELLA

Who what was? What?

DAVID

*(Impatient.)*

Which *critic* it was? From the *Times*.

ELLA

Oh! I don't know. . . .

DAVID

*(Incredulous.)*

You don't *know*?!

ELLA

I'm *sorry* . . .!

DAVID

You've gotta *know* these things, Ella—what's *wrong* with you?!
Jesus. . . .

*(Re: the web page on the iPhone.)*

Cocksucking *christ,* why's it *taking* so long?! Okay, here it is.

ELLA

Oh god. Oh *god.* . . .!

DAVID

*(Reading.)*

Sh. *Shhh* . . .!

> *Beat.*

> *Beat.*

> *He reads. He scrolls.*

> *Beat.*

ELLA

*(Dying with anticipation.)*

What's it *say* . . .?

DAVID

*(Reading; scrolling.)*

Hold on. Hold *on!*

ELLA

*(A terrified whisper.)*

I *can't* . . .!

DAVID

Man up. Man *up!*

ELLA

I'm *sorry!*

>    *Beat.*

DAVID

>    *(Reads.)*

Huh. Huh. . . .

ELLA

*What . . .?!*

>    DAVID *scrolls on the phone. He reads. He reads.*

DAVID

Yes. Yes. . . .

ELLA

Is it *good?!*

DAVID

Shut up!

>    DAVID *reads. He scrolls. He reads. He reads.*

>    ELLA *holds her breath.*

>    DAVID *reads. He scrolls. He reads. He reads. He finishes.*

DAVID

Okay.

ELLA

What's it say? What's it say?!

DAVID

It's good.

ELLA

It is? *It is?!*

DAVID

Yes.

ELLA

What else. What *else?!?*

DAVID

He liked it.

ELLA

Oh god. Oh *god* . . .!

DAVID

It's a rave.

*A tiny beat. Then—*

ELLA

*(Almost orgasmic.)*

OH MY GOD! OH MY GOD!! OH MY GOD!!! OH MY *GOD!!!!*

ELLA *jumps up and down.*

DAVID *laughs.*

ELLA *runs over to him and hugs him.*

*He hugs her back.*

DAVID

*(Softly, stroking her hair.)*

My baby. My baby. . . .

*He rocks her.*

*She cries.*

ELLA

I'm so *relieved* . . .!

DAVID

I know you are. I know you are. . . .

ELLA

Oh *god* . . .!

DAVID

Sit down. Sit down. . . .

ELLA

What . . .?

DAVID

*(Darkly.)*

There's something else. There's something else. . . .

*She sits.*

ELLA

*(Panicking.)*

What *is it?!?*

*A beat. Then—*

DAVID

It's a rave. . . for *her.*

*A beat.*

*Silence.*

*A beat.*

*Deadly.*

*A beat.*

*Then—*

ELLA

*(Crushed.)*

Oh god.

DAVID

*(Also crushed.)*

I know.

ELLA

*(In agony.)*

Oh *god.* . . .

DAVID

*(In agony, too.)*

I *know.* . . .

ELLA *starts to cry.*

ELLA

Am I mentioned . . . at *all* . . .?

*Beat.*

DAVID

In parentheses.

*She cries.*

ELLA

Oh *god* . . .!

DAVID

*(His heart breaking for her.)*

It's *okay.* . . .

ELLA

*(Just devastated.)*

It's *not!*

DAVID

Yes it *is!*

ELLA

*How . . .?!?*

    *Beat.*

DAVID

I don't know. . . .

ELLA

    *(Reaching for the phone.)*
Let me *see it!*

DAVID

You shouldn't. You absolutely shouldn't. . . .

    *He hands her the phone.*

    *She reads. She reads.*

ELLA

    *(In despair.)*
Oh my god.

DAVID

    *(Aching with compassion.)*
Sweetheart.

ELLA

    *(Reading; scrolling.)*
Oh . . . my . . . *god . . .!*

DAVID

    *(Watching her read.)*
*Sweetheart. . . .*

    *She reads, breathless.*

ELLA

    *(A mumble; scrolling.)*
Ohmygod . . . Oh my *god . . .!*

DAVID

It doesn't mean anything. It doesn't mean. . . *anything . . .!*

ELLA

Yes it does! *Yes it does . . .!*

DAVID

Well, that's true. In a way, that's true. . . .

> *She puts the phone down.*

ELLA

> *(Beginning to have trouble breathing.)*

Oh my god. Ohmygod.

DAVID

Are you all right?

ELLA

> *(Hyperventilating.)*

I can't *breathe . . .!*

DAVID

Here.

> DAVID *pours her another glass of wine. He brings the glass to her lips.*

DAVID

Drink this.

> ELLA *gulps it down.*

> *She drinks it like it's water.*

> DAVID *strokes her hair as she drinks.*

DAVID

Good. Good. . . .

> ELLA *gulps the wine.*

> DAVID *strokes her hair.*

> *She finishes drinking. Puts the glass down. She pants. Her eyes water. She stares at the glass.*

DAVID

> *(Stroking her hair; gently.)*

This is all material, you know. For when you write your first play.

ELLA

> *(Barely audible croak.)*

Dad. . . .

DAVID

What?

ELLA

I don't . . . *want* to . . . write a play. . . .

> *He strokes her hair.*

DAVID

*(Sweetly.)*
You say that now.

> *She takes one last sip of wine. She drains the glass. Puts the glass down. She pants. She pants.*

DAVID

How do you feel?

ELLA

I feel. . . tired. I feel. . . so tired. . . .

DAVID

It's okay. It's okay. . . .

> DAVID *reaches into his pocket and pulls out a baggie of cocaine.*

> *He empties some coke onto the table.*

ELLA

Oh good. Oh *good . . .!*

DAVID

Just hold on. Just holllllld onnn. . . *!*

ELLA

*(Desperately grateful.)*
Thank you. *Thank you.* . . .

> DAVID *takes out his wallet and removes a MetroCard and a dollar bill. Throws the dollar bill at* ELLA, *who starts to roll it up, as* DAVID *starts cutting up the cocaine with the MetroCard.*

DAVID

Here we go. Heeeere we go-o-o-o-o-o. . . .

ELLA

*(Slurring her words a bit.)*
Thankyousomuch. Thank you, thank you. . . .

> *He sings to* ELLA *as he cuts up the coke.*

DAVID

*(Sings.)*
"An ordinary day becomes a holiday . . .
When I'm with you. . . .

*I have lots of toys but I don't want to play . . .*
*When I'm with you. . . ."*

    *He finishes cutting up the coke.*

DAVID

    *(Cutting her off.)*
Okay, here you go—you go first.

ELLA

    *(Genuinely moved by his generosity.)*
Thanks, Dad. *Thanks.*

    ELLA *bends down and snorts a line of coke. She leans*
    *back and breathes in. Her eyes water.*

DAVID

Is it good?

    *She hands the rolled-up bill to her dad.*

ELLA

Yeah.

    DAVID *bends down and snorts a line of coke. He leans*
    *back and breathes in. His eyes water.*

DAVID

Oh yeah. Oh *yeah . . .!*

ELLA

That's good. That's *good . . .!*

DAVID

Oh my god. Oh my *god!*

ELLA

I feel better. I feel better!!!

DAVID

Me too. Me too!!!

    ELLA *snorts another line.*

ELLA

Oh my *god!*

    DAVID *snorts another line.*

DAVID

Holy *shit!*

ELLA

Oh *fuck!!*

DAVID

Give me a hug.

ELLA *hugs him.*

DAVID

Tighter. Tighter!

ELLA *squeezes tighter.*

ELLA

UNNNHHH!

*She releases. She hangs on him, loosely. They start to sort-of slow dance.*

ELLA

I love you.

DAVID

I know.

ELLA

I love you.

DAVID

I know.

ELLA

I love you.

DAVID

I know.

ELLA

I love you.

DAVID

I know.

*She pulls away from him.*

ELLA

Say you love me too.

DAVID

I love you too.

ELLA

Say it like you mean it.

DAVID

*(Kind of bouncing up and down.)*
I love you too I love you too I love you too!!!

ELLA                                      DAVID
*(Jumping up and down.)*          *(Sing-song-y.)*
I love you I LOVE YOU!!!!!!          Iloveyoutoo! Iloveyoutoo!!!

*We hear a* WOMAN'S VOICE *offstage:*

VOICE *(OS)*

GO TO BED!!!

*They laugh.*

ELLA                                      DAVID
*(Manically.)*                         *(Manically.)*
HAHAHAHAHAHAHAHA!!!        HAHAHAHAHAHAHAHA!!!

ELLA

*(To* DAVID.*)*

Mom!

DAVID

Hah!

ELLA

What an asshole!

DAVID

What a killjoy!

ELLA

*(Shouting offstage.)*
GO BACK TO BED, MOM!

DAVID

STOP RUINING OUR FUN!

*They giggle uncontrollably.*

MOM *(OS)*
Go to bed! You're keeping me *up* . . .!

ELLA

Just shut the door!

DAVID

Put some earplugs in!

ELLA

Turn the TV on!

DAVID

And shut up!

ELLA

Yeah, shut up!!!

> *They crack up.*

> *Sound of a door slamming offstage.*

DAVID

> *(Whispers to* ELLA.*)*

What a *cunt . . .!*

> *They giggle hysterically like naughty teenagers.*

> DAVID *pours more wine into both of their glasses.*

DAVID

> *(Musingly.)*

You look so much like her when she was your age. Before she got . . .
you know.

> *They laugh.*

DAVID

But you have her talent ten-fold. Because you're *mine,* too!

ELLA

> *(A side-splitting grin.)*

Thanks!

DAVID

She was never very good, anyway.

ELLA

Really?

DAVID

Oh sure. She *really* didn't know what to do with her hands. It's no
wonder she quit when she met me! She was scared. She was weak.
She shrank. She shirked. But you? Look at you. You . . . *go* for it.

ELLA

*(Gooey with gratitude.)*

*Thanks*, Dad!

*He smiles at her. Then—*

DAVID

But you gotta watch out.

ELLA

I do?

DAVID

Sure.

ELLA

Why?

DAVID

Because she's jealous. Because *everyone's* jealous. Jealous of you.

ELLA

*(Very dark.)*

No. . . . They're jealous of *Clementine*. . . .

DAVID

*(Also very dark.)*

. . . *Clementine* . . .!

ELLA

*(Nearly crying again.)*

She's the golden girl! Bertrand's little *favorite* . . .! She has the better part. She has the rave review. She has . . .

*(Near tears.)*

. . . *everything* . . .!

DAVID

Uch. Director's pet. That no-talent *twat*—she should be jealous of *you*!

ELLA

HAH.

DAVID

I'm not kidding! Why are you laughing? She *should*!

ELLA

*(Incredulous.)*

Why?!

DAVID

Because *she doesn't have what you have*, Ella! And she *never will.*

ELLA

Oh . . .?

DAVID

*You.*

ELLA

*(Misty-eyed.)*

Yes . . .?

DAVID

You're a *real artist.*

*She smiles. This means the world to her.*

ELLA

Thanks Dad.

*(Beat.)*

*Thanks.*

*He smiles at her. Then—*

DAVID

I'll never forget it. . . .

ELLA

What . . .?

DAVID

The night I found out about you!

ELLA

Oh . . .!

DAVID

I'd told your mother, before we got married, I didn't want kids. I'd said the same thing to Celia, when I married her. I was a middle-aged man when your mother and I met! And I knew, you know, 'cause of my rotten childhood, that I'd be a lousy father. And your mother agreed. And then one night—we were in our old apartment in Park Slope—and we were making love, and she looked up at me, and her eyes filled with tears—and she was just a kid herself at the time, and *beautiful,* back then—and she said, so afraid: "David? I'm pregnant." And Ella, I would've thought I'd be . . . so angry. I would've thought I'd hit the *roof . . .!* You know? But

you know what I did? I kid you not girlie—I burst into tears . . .!
Because I was happy.

>   *(Beat; remembers.)*

Because I was *happy*. . . .

ELLA

>   *(Deeply moved.)*

Oh Daddy. Dad. . . .

DAVID

>   *(Deeply moved, himself.)*

I . . . *love* . . . being a father. I had no idea. I had *no idea* . . .! I'd love
it. So much. . . .

>   *He touches her hand.*

ELLA

I love you, Dad.

>   *She clasps his hand.*

DAVID

Your mother getting sick is the best thing that ever happened to us.

ELLA

I know.

DAVID

It brought us *closer!*

ELLA

I *know!*

DAVID

And no one can take that away from us now.

ELLA

Right, Dad. *Right.*

>   *He smiles at her. Then—*

DAVID

I'm gonna miss you.

ELLA

What do you mean? When . . .?

DAVID

When you grow up. When you move out.

ELLA

Ohhh. . . .

DAVID

I'm gonna miss my little girl.

> ELLA *starts to cry.*

ELLA

Oh *Dad . . .!*

DAVID

Come here.

> *She moves closer to him. Snuggles up next to him.*
> *He strokes her hair.*

DAVID

My baby. My baby. . . .
> *(Kisses her hand.)*
My beautiful genius baby. . . .

ELLA

Oh Daddy. Oh Dad. . . .

> *They look at each other.*
> *A beat. Then—*

DAVID

You have a big blackhead.

ELLA

Where? *Where?*

DAVID

In your cheek!

ELLA

> *(Giggling.)*
Get it out. Get it out . . .!

> DAVID *digs his nails into* ELLA'S *cheek.*

DAVID

Ohhh . . . *yeah . . .!*

ELLA

Good. *Good.* . . .

DAVID

Got it!

                    ELLA
Show me. Show me!!!

    DAVID *holds out the tip of his finger to her.*

                    DAVID
Here.

                    ELLA
Wow . . .!

                    DAVID
I know . . .!

                    ELLA
Let's save it!!!

                    DAVID
Okay!

    *She takes the blackhead off his finger and gingerly places*
    *it on the table.*

                    ELLA
Lemme do you! Lemme do you!!!

                    DAVID
    *(Uneasy.)*
I don't know. . . .

                    ELLA
Please?! Please?!?

                    DAVID
    *(Relenting with a chuckle.)*
Okay. . . .

                    ELLA
    *(Clapping her hands with excitement.)*
Thank you!!!

    *She scans his face for blackheads.*

                    ELLA
I don't see any. . . .

                    DAVID
Oh really? Huh.

                    ELLA
Lemme see your back. Sometimes you have really big ones in your
back!

DAVID

*(Can't believe he's doing this.)*

Oh god! Okay. . . .

> *They stand up. He lifts his shirt up and turns around. She scans his back for blackheads.*

ELLA

*(Scanning.)*

Hm. Hmmm. . . .

DAVID

*(Chuckling at the absurdity of the situation.)*

Huh. Huh . . .!

ELLA

Oh my god. Oh. My. *God . . .!*

DAVID

*(Excited.)*

You found one?

ELLA

A *huge* one! A *HUGE* one!!!

DAVID

Well get it!

ELLA

*(Super excited.)*

Okay! Okay!!!

> *She digs her nails into his back.*

DAVID

OW!

ELLA

*(Still digging.)*

I'm sorry. I'm sorry. . . .

DAVID

It hurts!

ELLA

*(Digging, hard.)*

Well it's deep! It's *deep.* . . .

DAVID

*(Pulling away.)*

Ow! *Stop!*

ELLA

*(Imitating him; playful.)*

"Man up. Man *up!*" You fairy! You pansy! You *pussy!*

*He pulls away.*

DAVID

*(Cold.)*

What?

*Beat. He pulls further away.*

DAVID

*(Icy.)*

What?

*Beat. He turns his back to her.*

ELLA

*(Jovial.)*

It was a—joke . . .!

*He crosses to the table and picks up the ashtray.*

*A beat.*

ELLA

*(Scared; an attempt at humor.)*

Can't you take a—joke . . .?!

*He crosses to the trash and BANGS the ashtray against the trash can to empty it. Hard. He bangs it for a long time.*

ELLA

*(Really worried now.)*

. . . Dad . . .?

*He crosses back to the table, picks up the wine bottle, and begins to leave.*

ELLA

*(Frantic.)*

Dad . . .!

*Before he gets to the door—*

DAVID

You know she's fucking him, right?

*Beat.*

ELLA

Who?

DAVID

*(With a dark laugh.)*
You *know who.*

ELLA

Bertrand?!

*(Shakes her head—can't comprehend.)*
Clementine and. . . *Bertrand* . . .?

DAVID

Of course!

ELLA

He's married!

DAVID

So?!

ELLA

He's sixty-three years old!

DAVID

*(Laughs.)*
Holy *lord*, you're naive . . .!

ELLA

*(Thoroughly repulsed.)*
Why do you. . . think that? Why do you—

DAVID

Are you telling me you didn't you see them tonight? On that pathetic
excuse for red carpet? In that dismal press line? Are you telling
me you're *blind?* You have no *eyes?!* You didn't see how he put his
hand on the small of her back when they were being interviewed on
New York One. . . .

ELLA

*(Bewildered.)*
What . . .?

DAVID

And then later, when that joke of an artistic director was delivering one of her *endless* speeches, you didn't see how he whispered something in Clementine's ear and *licked* her earlobe . . .?

ELLA *blanches.*

ELLA

. . . *what* . . .?

DAVID

*(A big swig of wine from the bottle.)*

A man doesn't do that kind of thing unless he's regularly digging in a woman's snatch.

*He sits back down and lights a cigarette.*

*He swigs from the bottle.*

*A beat. Then—*

ELLA *suddenly RUNS over to the trash can, clutching her stomach, and DRY HEAVES into the trash.*

DAVID *doesn't react. He remains still, staring ahead darkly, blowing smoke rings. Swigging from the bottle.*

ELLA *DRY HEAVES several times—trying to vomit, but unable to.*

*She crouches on the ground, her head over the trash can, panting, spitting.*

DAVID

*(Singing to himself.)*

*"There's a place. . . for us. . . .*

*Somewhere. . . a place. . . for us. . . ."*

*He thinks. He smokes. She HEAVES.*

DAVID

*(Musingly.)*

You ever notice how when the 2/3 train takes off at Seventy-Second Street, it sings those first three notes? Something about how the wheels hit the tracks . . .?

*(He sings them.)*

Dah . . . *dah* . . . dah. . . .

*(Beat; smokes.)*

You ever notice that . . .?

> *She HEAVES.*

DAVID

I wonder if I'm the only one who's ever noticed that. . . .

> *She spits one last time into the trash can.*

> *Then—she gets up and returns to her seat, clutching her stomach, almost doubled over in pain.*

ELLA

> *(Clutching her head.)*

Oh my god! I had no *idea*. . . .

DAVID

You're so naive. You're like a little girl. . . .

ELLA

I'll be better. I'll be better.

DAVID

*Good.*

> *They sit in silence. Then—*

> DAVID *takes out the baggie of coke and snorts a bump off his pinkie nail.*

> *He hands the bag to* ELLA *and she takes it without even looking up.*

ELLA

> *(Dead voice.)*

Thanks.

> *She snorts a bump off her pinkie nail.*

> *They rub cocaine residue from the table on their gums.*

> *A beat. Then—*

ELLA

I feel depressed.

DAVID

I know.

> *A beat. Then—*

ELLA

> *(Tiny, scared voice.)*

Dad . . .?

DAVID

What.

ELLA

Should I just . . .

DAVID

*What?*

ELLA

Should I just. . . give up . . .?

DAVID *stares at* ELLA.

*A beat. Then—*

DAVID

"Give up?"

ELLA

*(Tiny, terrified voice.)*

. . . yeah . . .?

DAVID

Is that a real question?

ELLA

I-I don't know. Yeah . . .?

DAVID

*How could you, Ella? What would you do?!*

ELLA

Be a. . . doctor? Be a lawyer? Be a . . .

*(With distaste.)*

. . . dental hygienist . . .?

DAVID

*(With a vindictive laugh.)*

You'd be *terrible* at that!

ELLA

I know. . . .

DAVID

You'd be terrible at—*any of those things . . .!*

ELLA

I *know . . .!*

DAVID

You're good at *one thing*, Ella. And it's theater. It's *art*. That's it. That's *it!*

(*Beat.*)

And if you do anything else . . .? I'll fucking kill you with my bare hands.

ELLA

Dad.

DAVID

Because you know what you'd be doing? If you quit?

ELLA

What.

DAVID

You'd be fucking yourself over.

ELLA

Okay.

DAVID

You'd be fucking me over.

ELLA

Okay. . . .

DAVID

But worst of all? *Worst of all, Ella?* You'd be fucking the *American Theater over.*

*A beat. This sinks in.*

ELLA

Really . . .? *Really . . .?*

DAVID

*That's* how good you are, Ella. THAT's why you can't give up.

ELLA

(*Brightening.*)

Okay! *Okay . . .!*

DAVID

Do you want to fuck over Lanford Wilson?

ELLA

(*With a smile.*)

No. . . .

DAVID
*(With a smile, too.)*
Do you want to fuck over *August* Wilson?

ELLA
*(With a coy grin.)*
*No . . .!*

DAVID
*(Playfully.)*
Do you want to fuck over Eugene O'Neill? *Do you want to fuck over EUGENE O'NEILL?!?*

ELLA
*(Giggling uncontrollably.)*
No! *NO . . .!*

DAVID *laughs, too.*

DAVID
Good. *GOOD . . .!*

*They smile at each other. He smokes.*

*A beat. Then—*

DAVID
But you gotta get better parts.

*Beat. He puts out his cigarette.*

ELLA
*(Hangs her head.)*
I know. . . .

DAVID
No more "Masha"'s for you.

ELLA
I *know* . . .

DAVID
Why they asked you to read Masha in the first place is beyond me.

ELLA
I *know* . . .!

DAVID
You're a NINA!

ELLA

I KNOW!

DAVID

You'd *prepared* Nina.

ELLA

I *know.*

DAVID

I worked on it *with you!*

ELLA

I *know,* Dad. I *know!*

DAVID

Don't get testy with me.

ELLA

Sorry.

> *A beat.*

DAVID

I just don't understand it. . . .

ELLA

What . . .?

DAVID

You're so talented.

ELLA

Thanks. . . .

DAVID

You're so smart.

ELLA

Thanks!

DAVID

You're so *interesting.*

ELLA

*Thanks!*

DAVID

So *how come you're not a star?*

> *Beat.*

*Beat.*

*Beat.*

ELLA

*(She falls into despair.)*

I don't. . . know. . . .

ELLA *hangs her head.*

DAVID

*(Musingly; sing-song.)*

It's as raaandom and meaningless as the uuuuuuniverse. . .

DAVID *lights a new cigarette.*

DAVID

So you know what you gotta do?

ELLA *looks up.*

ELLA

What?

DAVID

You need to take your career into your own hands, El.

ELLA

Okay.

DAVID

Do the fucking, and stop getting fucked.

ELLA

*(Confused.)*

Okay. . . .

DAVID

Strap on a dick and fuck those cocksuckers 'til they scream!

ELLA

But *how . . .?!*

DAVID *grins.*

DAVID

*Write your own goddamn play.*

ELLA

Dad—

> DAVID

You wanna be a star? Write your *own* goddamn play! And *star* in it!

> *A beat. This sinks in.*

> ELLA

You think I could? You think I *could* . . .?

> DAVID

I know you could. I *know* you could . . .!

> ELLA
> *(The idea really sinking in.)*

I could write a play.

> DAVID

You could write a play.

> ELLA

I could *really* write a *play!*

> DAVID

You could *really write a play!*

> ELLA

And star in it!

> DAVID

And *star* in it!

> ELLA
> *(Giddy.)*

And it'll be a hit!

> DAVID
> *(With a proud smile.)*

And it'll be a *hit*.

> ELLA
> *(Thrilled.)*

And I'll be a *star . . .!*

> DAVID

And you'll be a star . . .!

> *(Beaming with pride.)*

And you'll be a *star*. . . .

> *They laugh.*

> *A beat. Then—*

ELLA *stops laughing. She looks suddenly very scared.*

                    ELLA

But Dad . . .?

                    DAVID
        *(Dreamily.)*
What . . .?

                    ELLA
        *(With real difficulty.)*
If I don't . . .

                    DAVID

What?

                    ELLA

If I don't—make . . .

                    DAVID
        *(Very impatient.)*
What! Spit it out. *What?!*

                    ELLA

If I don't make it?
        *(This is very hard for her.)*
Will you still love me . . .?
        *A beat.*
        *He smokes.*
        *She holds her breath.*
        *He exhales.*
        *She holds her breath.*
        *He takes a sip of wine.*
        *A beat.*
        *A beat. Then—*

                    DAVID

I will always love you.
        *She exhales.*

                    ELLA

Oh good! Oh *good* . . .!

                    DAVID

But I'll be very disappointed.

*Beat.*

ELLA
*(Devastated.)*
Oh *really* . . .?

DAVID
Of *course* . . .!

> *He puts out his cigarette. Gets up and heads to the bathroom, just offstage.*

ELLA
Oh *no*. . . .

> *(In despair.)*
> *She cries.*

DAVID
*(OS; singing the first three notes of "Somewhere" again.)*
Dah . . . *dah* . . . dah. . . .

> *A beat. She cries.*

ELLA
I want you to be proud of me.

> *Beat. We hear him begin to PEE.*

ELLA
I want you to think I'm doing great . . .!

> *Beat. He PEES.*

ELLA
Don't you think I'm doing okay . . .?!?

> *Beat. He PEES.*

ELLA
*(Desperately—manic.)*
I'm in a hit show off-Broadway! I'm Masha in *The Seagull!* With a huge avant-garde director at the helm! We do the whole play with no furniture—just velvet floors and gossamer curtains and wooden poles that we sanded ourselves! It's revolutionary! Dad! It's a hit! It's a *hit!!!*

> *The toilet FLUSHES. DAVID comes out of the bathroom.*

DAVID
*(Reticent.)*
I know. . . .

ELLA

But *what . . .?!?*

DAVID

("Isn't it obvious?")
You're not Nina.

*She weeps.*

DAVID

You're not the star. You're not a *star. . . .*

*She weeps.*

ELLA

I tried. I *tried . . .!*

DAVID

Did you?

ELLA

I thought it was mine. I worked so hard—remember? And I walked to
the audition and I knew—I just *knew* that Nina *was* mine! And then—

DAVID

And then.

ELLA

I saw her. In the waiting room.

DAVID

Yes.

ELLA

And I knew.

DAVID

You knew.

ELLA

I knew. It was hers.

DAVID

But no, but—see! *That's* your problem! *Right there!!!*

ELLA

What is?!

DAVID

You *gave* up!

ELLA

No! I still *tried . . .!*

DAVID

I don't believe you. I don't think you did.

ELLA

I did. I *did!*

DAVID

You gave up. In your *mind.*

ELLA

*(A desperate squeal.)*
*I had no choice! <u>She's better than me</u>!*

DAVID

*(A vicious hiss.)*
*No she's NOT, Ella!* Don't you *ever* think that! When you start to think they're winning?! <u>*That's when you die*</u>!

ELLA *weeps.*

ELLA

*(Sobbing into her hands.)*
. . . I know. . . I *know* . . .!

*He smokes.*

DAVID

I bet you didn't even audition for Nina. I bet you saw *her* in the waiting room and you just fucking surrendered, and you went in for Masha. I bet. *I bet.* . . .

*She cries harder.*

DAVID

Is that what happened?

*She bows her head.*

DAVID

*Is it?*

*She is silent.*

DAVID

*IS IT?!*

*She is silent. Avoids his gaze.*

*He looks at her. Repulsed.*

*A beat. Then—*

*He starts to laugh.*

DAVID

Hah. HAH! How'd I know. Howww'd I knnno-o-owwww. . . .

*He slowly stubs his cigarette out. He grinds it into the ashtray, hard.*

*A long, long, terrible beat.*

ELLA *weeps.*

*He is silent.*

*He lights another cigarette. He smokes.*

*She cries.*

DAVID

*(Darkly.)*

You know what this means, don't you?

*Beat.* ELLA *is silent.*

DAVID

You know what the lesson here is? *Don't you?*

*Beat.* ELLA *is silent.*

DAVID

*(With a shrug—it's obvious.)*

That she *is* better than you.

*Beat.*

ELLA

*(Tiny voice.)*

. . . what . . .?

DAVID

*(Eerily calm.)*

She went for it. She was brave. She had confidence. She had guts.
You were scared. You were weak. You shrank. You shirked. She won.
Congrats. You let her win. Hurray.

*A beat. He smokes. She cries.*

DAVID

*(Almost blasé.)*

Maybe you should just give up.

*A beat. He smokes. She cries.*

DAVID

*(An indignant snarl.)*

Don't bother writing a play. You'll just fuck that up too.

ELLA

*Dad. . . .*

> *He smokes.*
>
> *She looks at him.*
>
> *He doesn't look at her.*

ELLA

Dad . . .?!

> *He smokes.*
>
> *She looks at him.*
>
> *He doesn't look at her.*

ELLA

*(Desperate.)*

*Dad . . .!*

> *She runs over to him and tries to embrace him—flings herself on top of him, trying to get in his lap. He resists this, trying to push her away, but she is forceful.*

ELLA

*Daddy! DAD!*

DAVID

Get *AWAY from me!*

> *He SHOVES her off of him.*
>
> *She falls to the floor.*
>
> *She weeps on the floor.*
>
> *He smokes, and looks darkly in front of him, at nothing. She cries softly on the floor. He sings softly to himself.*

DAVID

*(Sings.)*

"*Someday. . . Somewhere. . . .*"

> *He smokes.*

                              DAVID
        *(Sing-song; almost cheerful.)*
"Nothing to be done. . . ."

        *She weeps hysterically on the floor.*

        *A beat.*

        *Then—*

        *She gets up.*

        *She wipes her eyes, her face.*

        *Then—*

        *She leaves.*

        *Silence.*

        DAVID *sits there, quietly smoking.*

        DAVID *smokes in silence.*

        *Many beats.*

        *Then—*

        *We hear footsteps approaching . . .*

        *A beat.*

        *Then—*

        ELLA *enters. She holds a suitcase.*

                              ELLA
I'm leaving.

                              DAVID
I know.

                              ELLA
Don't call me.

                              DAVID
Okay.

                              ELLA
I hate you.

                              DAVID
Who cares.

        *Silence.*

        *She stands there.*

*He smokes, his back to her.*

*She looks at him.*

*A beat.*

*Then—*

*She leaves.*

*A beat.*

*We hear a door opening and then slamming shut offstage.*

DAVID *puts out his cigarette.*

*A beat. Then—*

DAVID

Hmmm. . . .

*He pours himself a glass of wine.*

DAVID

*(Pouring.)*

Hmmmmmmmmmm. . . .

*(Talking to himself; sing-song.)*

What a night. . . . Whaaat a niiight. . . .

*(Takes a sip of wine; laughs to himself; sings.)*

"Toniiiiiight! Toniiight. . . ."

*He laughs to himself.*

*He gets up to empty the ashtray.*

*He starts to shake, ever so slightly.*

*He BANGS the ashtray against the trash can to empty it.*

*He bangs it over and over and over. Hard. Violently.*

*He can't stop.*

*He bangs.*

*Then—*

*The ashtray CRACKS APART in his hands.*

DAVID

Oh god. Oh god . . .

*He drops the shattered pieces of the ashtray in the garbage.*

*Looks at his hands, which are now BLEEDING.*

*He starts to shake.*

DAVID

*(Starting to cry.)*

Oh god . . .! Oh *god . . .!*

*He starts to sob. He gets on his knees.*

DAVID

*(Quietly.)*

Oh god. Oh *God!*

*He weeps and sobs.*

*He clasps his bleeding hands in prayer.*

DAVID

*(Softly.)*

Oh, God please help me. *God please help me!*

*He cries and cries.*

*Lights begin to fade.*

DAVID

God please help me. . . .

*Lights continue to fade as he repeats these four words in a desperate, strangled whisper.*

DAVID

God please *help me! God please help me!!!*

*Lights fade.*

*We can barely see him.*

DAVID

*(A last, desperate plea.)*

*God!*

*Blackout.*

END OF SCENE 1.

# SCENE 2

*Five years later.*

*An intimate black box theater. Late at night.*

*The set on stage is a replica of the kitchen from Scene 1: the same table, chairs, empty wine bottles, overflowing ashtrays, etc.*

*A ghost light stands center stage.*

*We hear a* WOMAN'S VOICE, *OS.*

> VOICE *(OS)*
>
> See that's what I'm talking about—they're ridiculous questions.

*The person behind the voice emerges:* ELLA. *But we would hardly know it—she looks and behaves almost like a different person. The nervous giddiness we saw in her before has been replaced with a steely assuredness. She carries herself with aggressive confidence and exudes an intimidating sex appeal.*

*She is extremely well-dressed in couture and heels. Her hair is sleekly blown out, her makeup flawless. She holds an expensive-looking large purse. She talks on her iPhone.*

> ELLA
>
> No you *don't* know, please—just let me finish.

*She plants her purse down on the stage and takes a seat as she continues to hold court on the phone.*

> ELLA
>
> They're the kind of questions posed by the kind of people who are completely petrified of their own existence. People who would rather swallow a bottle of *cyanide* than sit in a black box for ninety minutes and fucking *learn* some thing about themselves, am I right? I mean, the kind of theater these people want to see is something *safe*.

*She removes a bottle of wine from her bag—a small bottle of red, with a festive bow tied around its neck. She sets the bottle down on the stage.*

ELLA

They want a kitchen sink family drama! Not a metatheatrical one-woman show in which I play twelve different characters spanning three generations!

*She removes a different bottle of wine from her bag—a bottle of white.*

ELLA

These people just want to see the same shit that's been regurgitated in the American theater for decades. I mean it's like Stockholm syndrome! They actually think at this point that they *like* it! "Yes, please, more clichés!" "Please, more predictable jokes!" "Please, more wistfully hopeful, well-made endings! Please, oh please!"

*She finds a glass.*

ELLA

But that's the one thing I can't give them: something *safe*.

*(Takes a sip of wine.)*

I can give them pretty much anything but *safe*.

*She pours herself a glass of wine.*

ELLA

*(Laughs a little.)*

I mean, I don't mean to sound so self-*important*—I get it, I'm a solo performer, not Mother *Teresa*, but. . . .

*A beat. She listens to the person on the other end of the phone. Takes a sip of wine.*

ELLA

No, but—see! That's not the *point*. Whether it's "autobiographical" or not is not the—

*Beat.*

Okay, but what *I'm* saying is this: instead of asking yourself "Is this play a *factual retelling of real events that really happened in real life?*" Why don't you ask yourself something like this: "Did this play move me?" "Did I relate to it?" "Did some part of me wish I *hadn't* related to it?" These are the kinds of questions that I want my audience to—

*Beat. She hears something in her phone.*

ELLA

I'm sorry, I have another call. Can you hold?

*She presses a button on the phone.*

ELLA

I'm on my way, Shelly—I'll be there as soon as I—

*(Beat.)*

Can you hear me?

*(Beat; she moves.)*

How 'bout now?

*(Beat; she moves.)*

How 'bout now?

*(Beat; she moves.)*

How 'bout now?!

*(Beat.)*

Okay great. I'll be there as soon as I can.

*(Beat.)*

I thought it went okay. I mean, that last grandfather letter and some
of the Shirley Temple stuff still feels terrible and I feel like a fucking
hack when I'm doing it, but—

*(Beat.)*

A fucking hack? When I'm *doing* it?

*(Beat.)*

Never mind, Shelly—I'll see you there soon. Oh, and tell the photog-
raphers I'm on my way. Bye.

*She presses a button on the phone.*

ELLA

Hi, are you still there?

*(Beat.)*

Oh great. I was worried I'd lose you because the service down
here is so terrible. Anyway, as I was saying: *these* are the kinds of
questions that I want my audience to—

*(Beat. She hears something in her phone.)*

ELLA

I'm sorry, I have another call. Can you . . .? Thanks.

*She presses a button on the phone.*

ELLA

What do you want, you stupid fucking bitch?

*(Beat; then, laughs.)*

Just kidding! Hiiiiii . . .!

*(Beat.)*

Oh my *god* yes I got it—you are *soooooo* sweet.

*She picks up the small bottle of red wine. Examines the label.*

ELLA

Mmm . . . from Côtes du Rhône. . . . So *yummm . . .!*

*She gets up and throws the bottle of wine in the trash. Laughs at something the other person is saying.*

ELLA

No, stop.

*(Beat; laughs.)*

No, *stop . . .!*

*(Beat; peeved now.)*

No, actually stop, 'cause I do have to run. I'm on the other line actually with—

*(Beat.)*

Okay, great. Oh, and congrats on St. Louis! Regional theater is *so* fun.

*(Beat.)*

Okay, you too, Clementine. Mwa mwa.

*She presses a button on the phone.*

ELLA

Hi, are you still there? Okay, great. Now, as I was saying: *these* are the kinds of questions that—

*Beat. She hears something in her phone.*

ELLA

I'm *so* sorry, I have another—thanks.

*She presses a button on her phone.*

                         ELLA

What is it, Shelly?

    *(Beat.)*

Well, what the fuck are they gonna do? Leave the Opening Night party before I show up?! I'm the writer, director and *only actor in the play.*

    *(Beat.)*

No, I *don't want to know—*

    *(Beat.)*

Because I don't read them anymore!

    *(Beat.)*

I'm not *kidding,* Shelly—even if it's the best review you've ever read? In your entire career as an agent? *Ever?* I am truly not kidding. I *don't want to know.*

    *She presses a button on the phone.*


                         ELLA

Hi, are you still there? Okay great. Here's what I want to say: the thing about my work—the thing that's—

    *(Beat.)*

No, I wouldn't say that—

    *(Beat.)*

Because it's *not* about him! It's about—

    *(Beat; a sudden eruption.)*

*Don't interrupt me.*

    *(Beat; attempting a more measured tone.)*

I wouldn't say that. We *have* a good relationship. We just don't speak.

    *A beat. She listens to the person on the other end. Then—*


                         ELLA

    *(Sweetly.)*

I'm sorry, can you hold on just one minute?

    *She puts the phone down. Picks up her glass of wine. Chugs. Chugs.*

    *A beat. Then—*

    *She picks up the phone.*

ELLA

Thank you so much. Now. As I was saying: the thing about my work —the thing that's *always* been true about my—

*A beat. She listens. Then—*

ELLA

(*Icy.*)

What kind of a fucking question is that?

(*Beat; venomous.*)

Does it *look* like I'm suffering now? Does it *look* like I have any goddamn "*regrets?*" *Every* thing I did—*every* decision I made—led me *right here*—*right to this moment*, here with *you.* If I hadn't done all that—if none of that shit had never happened? I never would've written "In Parentheses"! I never would have—

*She presses a button on the phone.*

ELLA

FUCK YOU SHELLY!

*She presses a button on the phone.*

ELLA

I never would have—

(*Beat.*)

Oh. You do? Aw, that's too bad. Are you sure you got everything you need?

(*Beat.*)

Okay. Well. Great! And when do you think the article will run?

(*Beat.*)

Oh, this Sunday. Amazing. And will I get approval of the *photo* that you're going to—

(*Beat.*)

Uh-huh. Okay. Great. And will it be *above* the fold? Or—

(*Beat.*)

Uh-huh. Uh-huh. Well, I hope so, too. And—

(*Beat.*)

Hello?

(*Beat.*)

*Hello?*

*She looks at her phone. Realizes the call has ended.*

ELLA

*(Muttering to herself.)*

Fucking service down here is terrible. . . .

*She puts her phone down; picks up the bottle of wine and pours herself a new glass.*

*She takes a sip of wine.*

*Rolls her shoulders back.*

ELLA

Hmmm. . . .

*She takes a sip of wine. Rolls her head around.*

ELLA

Hmmmmmmmmm. . . .

*A beat. Then—*

*She opens her purse. Begins to rummage around inside. Sings to herself as she does this.*

ELLA

*(Sings; a little girl's voice.)*

"Animal crackers in my soup. . . ."

*She removes a small cosmetics pouch. Takes out a compact. Examines her face in the mirror.*

ELLA

*(Muttering to herself.)*

I look fucking terrible.

*She begins to reapply her makeup.She takes out an eyelash curler. Curls her eyelashes.*

*As she does this, she talks out loud to herself, running lines from her show.*

ELLA

*(Russian accent.)*

"My darling son. Hello, again. I feel foolish to continue to write you these letter, but I do not know what else I can do. I am like Tantalus —I keep . . ."

*She puts the eyelash curler back and removes a tube of lipstick; touches up her lipstick.*

ELLA

*(Russian accent.)*

"My darling son. Hello, again. I feel . . ."

*(Tries that word again, working on the accent.)*

"I feel. . . ."

*(Beat.)*

"I feel. . . ."

*She trails off. A beat. Then—*

ELLA

*(Out of character; muttering under her breath.)*

This is fucking terrible.

*She puts the lipstick and compact back in her pouch. Puts the pouch back in her purse.*

*She takes a big gulp of wine. Opens her purse, and retrieves a pot pipe from her purse.*

*She lights it. She inhales. She holds the pot in her lungs. Exhales.*

*She gets quiet. And then—*

*She begins to get into character: she hunches her back; her eyelids become heavy; she seems suddenly much, much older—and masculine. Her left hand shakes with a tremor.*

ELLA

*(Russian accent.)*

"My darling son. Hello, again. I feel foolish to continue to write you these letter, but I do not know what else I can do. I am like Tantalus —I keep reaching for grape, but I know they always be out of reach.

*(Beat.)*

But I write, and keep reaching, and pray, to hope that you one day my boy decide to open his father letter and not to mail back."

*Her performance is beautiful—simple, heartbreaking.*

ELLA

*(Russian accent.)*

"I wish you let me be you father again. I know you angry—I am angry

too, at myself. You old dad always have trouble with this anger—this
sticky, mean monster, that chew up so many great men. . . ."

*A beat. Then—*

ELLA
*(Muttering to herself; out of character.)*
I'm a fucking hack.

*She get up and crosses to the ashtray. Dumps the residue
from the pipe into it. Then, she picks up the ashtray, and
crosses to the trash can. She BANGS the ashtray against
the trash can to empty it.*

*She bangs it over and over and over. Hard. Violently.*

*Then—*

*She stops.*

*She stands over the trash can, panting.*

*A beat.*

*A beat.*

*Then—*

*A sudden BURST of light—a door opens—the door to the
theater.*

ELLA *WHIPS around, terrified.*

*A figure stands in the doorway, silhouetted by the light
from the lobby.*

*A beat. Then—*

*The figure emerges.*

*It is* DAVID.

*The door closes behind him.*

*A beat.*

*Darkness, now, aside from the ghost light.*

ELLA *looks at her father.*

*The blood drains from her face as she takes him in.*

*He looks very different from the last time we saw him. He
is more hunched—he seems much smaller.*

*His face is gray. The lines in his face are deeper. He looks
exhausted, like he has been though a war. He looks like
he has aged a hundred years.*

*Still, it is clear he has put a considerable effort into his appearance—he is cleaned up: he wears a suit and tie. His hair is combed. He holds a small bouquet of roses. His eyes are clear. He looks at* ELLA.

*She looks at him.*

*A long, long silence.*

ELLA *is paralyzed.*

*A beat. Then—*

ELLA

Oh my *god*. . . .

*She takes him in. A beat. Then—*

*She suddenly BURSTS out laughing. Manically. Hysterically.*

ELLA

You're *so* . . . OLD . . . !

*She cracks up.*

*Beat.*

*She stops laughing.*

ELLA

*(Really taking him in.)*

You look . . . *so* . . . old. . . .

*Beat.*

*She takes him in.*

ELLA

*(Becoming upset.)*

You look . . . dead. . . .

*Beat.*

ELLA

Are you . . . *dead* . . . ?

*A beat.* DAVID *is completely silent. He just looks at* ELLA; *smiles, sadly.*

*She starts to panic.*

ELLA

*(Starting to tremble.)*

What's—*wrong* . . . ?!

DAVID *opens his mouth to speak—*

DAVID

. . . . . . . . .

ELLA
*(Very alarmed.)*
W-what . . .?

DAVID
I . . . laaahve . . .

*His speech is thick—slurred, labored. He has extreme difficulty getting the sounds out.*

*He clears his throat. Begins again.*

DAVID
I . . . *laaahve* . . . yooouuu . . . Ehl-lahhh. . . .

*Beat. She starts to shake.*

ELLA
What . . .?!?

*He clears his throat.*

DAVID
*(Trying very hard to articulate.)*
I . . . *hahd* . . . a *strohhhke.* . . . I'm . . . *ohhh*-kay. . . . but . . . it's . . . haaahhh-hd . . . fohr . . . meee. . . to . . .

*(He sings the next word.)*
. . . *speeeeeeeaaaaaak.* . . .

ELLA *is silenced. Just looks at him. Paralyzed.*

*A beat. Then—*

*He continues to speak-sing. The tune is "Somewhere," from "West Side Story."*

DAVID
*(Explaining; singing.)*
It's . . . *eeeas-i-er* . . . when . . . I . . . *siiiiing.* . . .

*(Beat.)*
My . . . speech . . . der-a-pist . . . tehlls . . . me . . . tooo . . . *siiiing* . . .

*(Beat.)*
. . . *whaaaht* . . . I . . . *waaahhhnt* . . . to . . *saaayyy* . . .

*(Beat.)*
Dat's . . . dee . . . *ohhhn-ly* . . . *waaaaaay*—

*He is cut off by a sob. He tries to hold it in.*

*He cries.*

ELLA *is paralyzed.*

*She stares at him.*

*A beat. Then—*

*She begins to gather her things.*

ELLA

*(Softly.)*

It's really late. What am I doing here. I have to go. . . .

*David stands there, watches her, blinks—he looks almost calm—tranquil even; almost serene.*

*A beat. Then—*

DAVID

*(Singing to the tune of "Somewhere")*

*(Beat.)*

An . . . impohhhrtant . . . paaahrt . . .

*(Beat.)*

. . . ahhhv . . . de . . . reeeeeeeeeeeeeeeeeeeee . . . cohverrrry . . .

*(Beat.)*

. . . proh-cess . . . is . . . maaaykeeen . . . ahhhm-ennnnds . . .

*(Beat.)*

. . . tooooo . . . dohhhse . . . I've . . . haaahrmed. . . .

*(Beat.)*

I . . . ohhhwe . . . youu . . . an . . . ahhhmends. . . .

*(Beat.)*

I . . . wahs . . . a . . . bad . . . fahhh-derrrr. . . .

*(Beat.)*

I . . . diiih-dn't . . . giiihve yooou . . . da . . . laaahve . . .

*(Beat.)*

. . . dat . . . yooou . . . deee-zerrrhrve. . . .

ELLA *looks at her father, in deep pain and horrified fascination.*

DAVID

I . . . wahhhs . . . sehhhl-fiiish. . . .

*(Beat.)*

I . . . wahhhs . . . dis-haaahn-est. . . .

    *(Beat.)*

I . . . wahhhs . . . ihhhn-con-siiiiiderate. . . .

    *(Beat.)*

I . . . wahhhs . . . ahhh-fraaayd. . . .

    *(Beat; he chokes back a sob.)*

I'm . . . graaayt-ful . . . fohr . . . my . . . strrrohhhke. . . .

    *(Beat.)*

It . . . maaayde . . . meee . . . aaasssk . . . fohr . . . hehhhlp. . . .

    *(Beat.)*

I . . . wahhhs . . . liiiving . . . al-ohhh-ne . . . up-staaay-te . . .

    *(Beat.)*

. . . driiinking . . . my-sehhlf . . . tooo . . . dehhhttt. . . .

    *(Beat.)*

Dis . . . strohhhke . . . saaayved . . . my . . . liiife. . . .

    *(Beat.)*

Da . . . daaahc-tors . . . saiiid . . . tooo . . . meee. . . .

    *(Beat.)*

"If . . . you . . . dohhhn't . . . goh . . . to . . . A . . . A . . .

    *(Beat.)*

. . . youuu . . . wiiilll . . . die. . . .

    *(Beat; laughs a little.)*

I . . . said . . . "I'd . . . raaa-der . . . die". . . .

    *(Beat; laughs; shrugs.)*

I . . . showhhhd . . . up . . . annny-waaay . . .

    *(Beat.)*

. . . gaaahhht . . . a spohhhn-sor . . . and wohhhrked . . . da . . . steps. . . .

    *(Beat.)*

My . . . liiife . . . beee-gannn . . . tooo . . . chaaaynge. . . .

    *(Beat.)*

I've . . . bihhhn . . . s-ohhh-ber . . . fohhhr . . .

    *(Beat.)*

. . . twooo . . . ahhhnd . . . a . . . hahhh-lf . . . yeeears. . . .

*(Beat.)*

*My . . . liiife . . . hahs . . . gaaahhhten . . . riiihhhch . . . and . . . fuuuhhhl. . . .*

*(Beat; with emotion.)*

*I . . . hahve . . . fouuunnnd . . . my . . . hohhhmmm. . . .*

*(Beat.)*

*Ehhhvry . . . mohhhrniiing . . . I . . .*

*(Beat.)*

*. . . gehhht . . . on . . . my . . . kneees . . . and . . . saaayyy . . .*

*(Beat.)*

*"Gohhhd . . . pleeease . . . shohhhw . . . me . . . yohhhr . . . wiiihhhlll . . . tooodaaayyy. . . .*

*(Beat.)*

*Shohhhw . . . meee . . . hohhhw . . . tooo . . . beee. . . ."*

*(Beat; he smiles.)*

*Den . . . I . . . saaayyy . . . "Gohhhd . . .*

*(Beat; choking back tears.)*

*. . . pleeease . . . giiiiiiiiiiiiiiive . . . Ehl-lahhh . . .*

*(Beat.)*

*. . . everrryyyyyyyting . . . daaat . . . sheee . . . deserrrves. . . .*

*(Beat.)*

*. . . Hehhhlp . . . herrr . . . tooo . . . beee . . . freeeeee. . . ."*

*(Beat; smiles, through tears.)*

*I . . . reahhhd . . . ahhhbout . . . yohr . . . shohhhw. . . .*

*(Beat.)*

*I . . . am . . . ah-maaayzed . . . by . . . yooouuu. . . .*

*(Beat.)*

*Yooouuu . . . ahhhre . . . feeearless . . . and . . . yooouuu . . . ahhhre . . . strohhhng. . . .*

*(Beat; beams, through tears.)*

*An . . . aaahhhr-tist . . . I . . . ad-miiihre. . . .*

*(Beat.)*

*Yooouuu . . . ahhhre . . . dooo-eeehng . . . graaayt. . . .*

*(Beat; glowing.)*

*Yooouuu . . . ahhhre . . . dooo-eeehng . . . graaayt. . . .*

   *(Beat; with great emotion.)*

*Yooouuu . . . ahhhre . . . dooo-eeehng . . . sohhh . . . graaayt. . . .*

   *(Through tears.)*

*I'm . . . soh . . . prouuud . . . of . . . youuuu . . .!*

   ELLA *listens.*

   DAVID *cries. Clears his throat. Continues.*

DAVID

*I . . . knohhhw . . . dat . . . diiis . . . is . . . hahhhrd. . . .*

   *(Beat.)*

*I . . . knohhhw . . . dat . . . yooouuu . . . ahhhre . . . scaaayred. . . .*

   *(Beat.)*

*I-I-I . . . am . . . scaaayred . . . tooooo . . .*

   *(Smiling, through tears.)*

*I'm . . . ahhhl-so . . . soh . . . haaapy . . . tooo . . . seeeeeee . . . yooouuu. . . .*

   *Slowly, tentatively, he moves toward her.*

DAVID

Saaahhhm . . . daayyyy. . .

   *Slowly, tentatively, he moves closer.*

DAVID

Saaahhhhm . . . whehhhre . . .

   *She lets him approach her. He keeps singing.*

DAVID

Weee'll . . . fiiind . . . a . . . neeew . . . waaayyy . . . of . . . liiiveeehng. . .

   *Ever so gingerly, he places his hand on her arm.*

   *Ever so slightly, she starts to smile at him.*

   *Ever so softly, he continues to sing, and ever so delicately, she begins to join in as* DAVID *leans in to embrace her.*

| DAVID | ELLA |
|---|---|
| Weee'll . . . fiiind . . . a . . . waaayyy . . . of . . . fohr-giiiv-y eeehng. . . . | Weee'll . . . fiiind . . . a . . . waaayyy of . . . fohr-giiiv-eeehng . . . |

   *And suddenly—she SHOVES past him.*

*He stumbles.*

*She crosses to her bag, reaches inside and pulls out a baggie of cocaine.*

*He turns, and sees.*

*She shoves her finger into the baggie and snorts some coke off her pinkie nail.*

DAVID *approaches her, gently. He gingerly places a hand on her shoulder.*

*As his hand touches her shoulder. . .*

ELLA

Get *AWAY from me!*

*She SHOVES him off her.*

*He falls to the floor.*

*She looks at him, lying on the floor. Then—*

*She picks up the wine bottle, and slowly, deliberately, POURS the rest of the bottle of wine on his face.*

*He doesn't move. Doesn't even make a sound. He just accepts it.*

*Then—She turns away. Slams the now-empty wine bottle down on the table. Sits back down in* DAVID*'s chair. She lights a cigarette. Inhales deeply.*

DAVID *begins to get himself up—slowly, laboriously. He has much trouble moving.*

ELLA *doesn't react. She remains still, staring ahead darkly, smoking.*

DAVID *heads for the door.*

ELLA *blows smoke rings.*

DAVID *reaches the door. He stands in the doorway.*

ELLA *blows smoke rings.*

DAVID *stands in the doorway.*

ELLA *doesn't look.*

*A beat. Then—*

*He leaves.*

*A beat.*

*We hear a door opening and then slamming shut offstage.*

*A beat. Then—*

ELLA

Hmmm. . . .

*She stands up and crosses to the trash. Her movements are wobbly, jerky. She leans over the trash, and searching through it with her hands. Picks out the smaller bottle of wine. Looks at it.*

ELLA

Hmmmmmmmmmm. . . .

*She slowly pulls the gold ribbon off the wine—sees that it's a screw-top. Throws the ribbon on the floor; unscrews the top, and throws it on the floor. Then—*

*She crosses to the back wall of the theater. She leans against a wall, clutching the bottle.*

ELLA

Nothing to be done. . . .

*A beat. Then—*

*She brings the wine bottle to her lips and CHUGS.*

*She slowly slides down the wall, the bottle glued to her lips.*

*She chugs and chugs. She sits on the floor. She takes a drag off her cigarette. She puts it out on the floor. Then—*

*She takes the baggie of cocaine out of her pocket and shoves two fingers inside. She shovels cocaine into her nose. She snorts it like a pig. She chugs more wine. Finishes the bottle.*

*A beat. Then—*

*She lies down.*

*Lies there. Motionless.*

*A beat.*

*A beat.*

*A beat.*

*Then—*

*Her PHONE RINGS.*

*A beat. Then—*

*She stands up. Wobbily rummages around to find her phone. Picks it up.*

ELLA

*(Woozily.)*

. . . h-hello-o. . . .

*(Beat; very quiet, eyes closed.)*

I'm resting. . . .

*She opens her eyes. Listens. A beat. Then—*

ELLA

*(Suddenly filled with fury.)*

I fucking TOLD you Shelly I don't want to know! I *don't want to know!* *I DON'T WANT TO KNOW!! I DON'T WANT TO KNOW!!! I DON'T WANT TO KNOW!!! I DON'T WANT TO KNOW!!! I DON'T WANT TO KNOW!!! I DON'T WANT TO KNOW!!! I DON'T WANT TO KNOW!!! I DON'T WANT TO KNOW!!!*

*(A vicious hiss.)*

Because when you start to think they're winning?! <u>*That's when you die!*</u>

*She hangs up.*

*Slams the phone down on the table.*

*She pants.*

*She stares at the phone.*

*She pants.*

*Then—*

*She picks up the wine bottle from the floor.*

*She chugs.*

*She picks up the baggie of cocaine from the floor. Shoves her fingers inside and snorts some coke off her fingers.*

*A beat.*

*She looks at her phone.*

*A beat.*

*A beat.*

*Then—*

*She picks up the phone. Types something in.*

ELLA

*(Muttering to herself.)*

It's loading. It's loading. . . .

*(Beat.)*

Oh god. . . . Oh *god* . . .!

*(Looks at her phone; mutters.)*

Cocksucking *christ*, why's it *taking so long* . . .?!

*Eyes still glued to the phone, she chugs from the bottle. Rubs some cocaine residue on her gums.*

*She looks at her phone.*

*A beat. Then—*

ELLA

Okay, here it is.

*(Scrolls, reads.)*

Oh god. Oh *god*. . . .!

*(Reading.)*

Sh. Shhh . . .!

*Beat. Beat.*

*She reads. She scrolls.*

*As she reads, she transforms. She becomes* DAVID, *and* ELLA—*switching off.*

ELLA

What's it say? What's it *say* . . .?

*(Reading; scrolling.)*

Hold on. Hold *on*!

*(A terrified whisper.)*

I can't. *I can't* . . .!

*(Beat.)*

Man up. Man *up*!

*(In agony.)*

I'm sorry. I'm *sorry* . . .!

*(Reads.)*

Huh. Huh. . . .

*(Beat.)*

What. *What . . .?!*

> ELLA *scrolls on the phone.*
>
> *She reads. She reads.*

ELLA

It's good. It's good. . . .
It is?! *It is?!*
Yes. Yes. . . .
What else. What *else?!?*
He liked it. He liked it . . .!
Oh god. Oh *god . . .!*
It's a rave. It's a rave!

> *A tiny beat. Then—*

ELLA

*(Almost orgasmic.)*

OH MY GOD! OH MY GOD!! OH MY GOD!!! OH MY *GOD!!!*

> *A transcendent, glowing smile seems to overcome her whole being.*

ELLA

*(On another plane of existence.)*

It's a rave—for *you.*

> *She beams. She beams.*
>
> *A beat.*
>
> *She looks out at the theater—the empty seats.*
>
> *A beat.*
>
> *A beat. Then—*

ELLA

*(Dreamily.)*

It's a hit. It's a hit . . .!

> *Beat.*

ELLA

I'm a star. I'm a star . . .!

> *A beat. Then—*
>
> *Her face falls.*

ELLA

It's a hit.

*She begins to cry.*

ELLA

I'm a star.

*She cries.*

ELLA

I'm a star.

*She cries.*

ELLA

*(In despair.)*
I'm a *star . . .!*

*She gets on her knees.*

ELLA

Oh god . . .! Oh *God . . .!*

*She clasps her hands in prayer.*

ELLA

Oh, God please help me. . . .

*Lights fade as she repeats these four words in a desperate, strangled whisper.*

ELLA

God please *help* me! *God please help me!!!*

*We can barely see her.*

ELLA

*(A last, desperate plea.)*
*God!*

*Blackout.*

*END OF PLAY.*